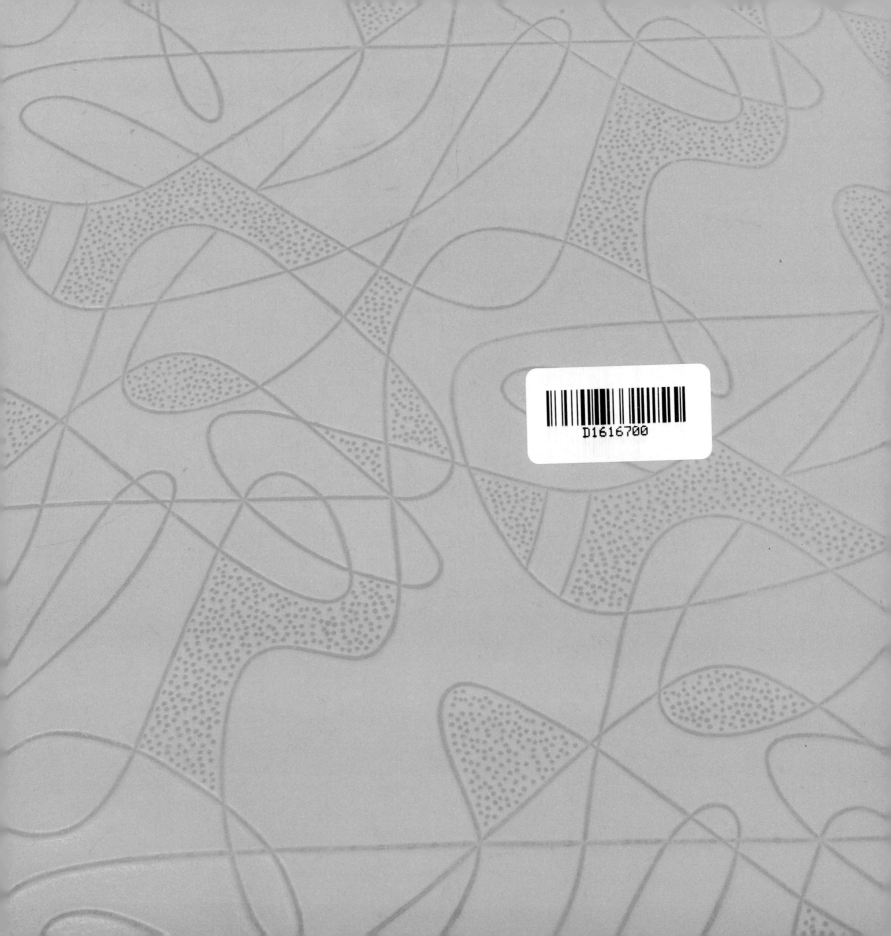

atomic RANCH

atomic RANCH

DESIGN IDEAS FOR STYLISH RANCH HOMES

Michelle Gringeri-Brown

Photographs by Jim Brown

Gibbs Smith, Publisher
SALT LAKE CITY

First Edition
10 09 08 07 06 5 4 3 2

Published by
Gibbs Smith, Publisher
P.O. Box 667
Layton, Utah 84041

Orders: 1.800.748.5439
www.gibbs-smith.com

Designed by Deibra McQuiston
Printed and bound in China

Library of Congress Cataloging-in-Publication Data
Gringeri-Brown, Michelle.
 Atomic ranch : design ideas for stylish ranch homes / Michelle Gringeri-Brown;
photographs by Jim Brown.—1st ed.
     p. cm.
 Includes index.
 ISBN 1-4236-0002-9
 1. Ranch houses—United States. 2. Architecture—United States—20th century.
I. Title.

NA7208.G75 2006
728'.3730973-dc22

2006004614

Contents

Introduction 6

Inspiring Originals 8

Is My House a Ranch? 40

Stunning Transformations 52

Modest Makeovers 88

Pure Fun 108

Outside the Ranch 136

Adding Personality 152

Preserving Midcentury Neighborhoods 176

Ranch Resources 190

Introduction

ARCHITECTURE'S UNDERDOG

A ranch house? Are you kidding me? Those homes are ugly.

If you're house hunting or live in one of the millions of ranches built across the nation after World War II, you've probably heard a sentiment like that from one of your less tactful friends. Maybe you even think so too.

But this book shows that there's more to America's architectural stepchild than first meets the eye. You say they don't have the curb appeal of a Victorian or bungalow? That their attached carports and garages and sometimes bland facades don't really do it for you?

Well, come inside a ranch house that still shows its midcentury roots and you'll see why fifty years ago young homeowners found them to be cutting edge and their own piece of Tomorrowland.

The open floor plans that bring residents together in the kitchen/family/dining/living room foreshadowed today's ubiquitous "great rooms," yet were designed on a livable, human scale. The private bedroom wings, the walls of glass that flood the interior with light, and the sliding glass doors that erase the barrier between indoors and out—these are other hallmarks of the late-'40s through 1970s ranch. Durably built with materials that combine the natural (wood post-and-beam construction, aggregate and cork flooring, rock roofs and stone fireplaces) with the modern (Formica counters, radiant heated concrete floors, aluminum windows, plywood cabinetry)—these postwar homes may not look flashy but they were designed to last.

The homes may be decidedly modern looking, like the flat- or gable-roofed Joseph Eichler tracts in the San Francisco Bay area, or the butterfly roof houses in Palm Springs and Sarasota, Florida. Or they may be modest, unassuming L-shaped or split-level ranches that have been built so often across the nation that they're virtually invisible. You probably drive past dozens of such homes on your way to work every day.

We think that the midcentury ranch house deserves a place of honor in our hearts and minds, and we think that postwar neighborhoods should be preserved for the next generation. Buying, renovating, and living in a ranch-style home can be a great joy, and we'll show you inspiring examples of people who "get" what a ranch house was designed to be. This mousey little wallflower of a home may very well be the stuff of your dreams.

Here's to the bad boy of architecture.

Inspiring Originals

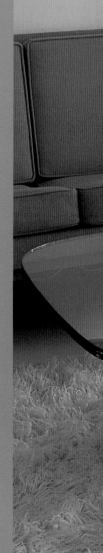

Dive into wonderful homes that showcase original midcentury details, architecturally appropriate renovations, and inspired furnishings. Their homeowners love vintage and contemporary modern, making for a personalized take on stylish living.

Eichler Two-Timers

When the homeowners arrived on moving day, the front of the house was completely exposed. After the renovation, the flat-roof Eichler looks pristine and original.

Monika Kafka and Tom Borsellino had already lived in this San Jose neighborhood before relocating to Chicago. But work and a hankering for the sunny, casual California lifestyle pulled them back. Borsellino found a house and bought it with his wife's blessing but without her actually seeing it. He told her it needed a little work, and an early inspection indicated some dry rot and termite damage. Mostly it seemed to be suffering from claustrophobic '60s-meets-Asian decor.

When the couple, with a two-year-old and two-month-old in tow, pulled up to move into the house, the front facade had been stripped down to the insulation, and the baby's room was completely open to the street. It was 105 degrees outside, but an even more stunning 108 degrees inside. Kafka was not charmed. In all, 90 percent of the distinctive grooved Eichler siding needed replacing, and while the walls were open, the couple opted to insulate and ground the electrical system. Although the roof was only four years old, they decided to install operable skylights in several rooms and replace the black tar and gravel with an insulating foam roof, which Borsellino estimates has cooled off the house 15 to 20 degrees.

The construction crew had found substantial damage in most of the posts and some of the beams, and awaited Borsellino's directions on what he wanted to do—as if he had an option. The original kitchen cabinets were painted a sickly harvest gold, and Borsellino's first inclination—though one that runs counter to his preservationist tendencies—was to rip it out. But with the huge structural job they had fallen into, the kitchen's aesthetics were the least of their worries.

"From late summer on, three to five guys were here every day," Kafka says. She

our previous Eichler *was the beta plan for this later model;*

this house is **much more functional.**

The refrigerator is one of the few new elements in the lightly renovated kitchen. With the mustard-color paint replaced with crisp black, and the fretwork room divider removed, the original white laminate counters, built-in Thermador wall oven, and mahogany wall paneling look very today.

became adept at feeding the crew and facilitating any construction snags while juggling the kids' needs. "But by April it was my house again," she says.

Instead of slate, bamboo, or hardwood flooring, the couple settled on vinyl composite tile from Armstrong as a good, affordable option—$4,000 versus $24,000 for slate—and the closest to the tract's original 9-inch asbestos floor tiles. Some of the original mahogany paneling had faded or was beyond repair; Borsellino used a combination of Watco Golden Oak and Fruitwood with some orange universal colorant mixed in to match new pieces to the existing. In the kitchen, they simply painted the cabinets black and found they liked the kitchen just fine that way. The baths were a different matter, though.

"Joseph Eichler didn't think out the baths in these houses," Borsellino says, "so I have no problem making changes. They ran the same mahogany paneling from the bedroom into the bath and tiled

right on top of it. Of course they're all full of dry rot and termite damage by now." Taking a clue from the one-inch tile on the shower floor, they installed glass mosaic tile throughout the toilet and shower area and added a skylight to brighten up the small room.

The couple furnished with a mix of vintage, modern reissues, and inexpensive kid-proof furniture from IKEA. "The 'dog-bone' sofa is from Modernica and the Saarinen table with the lazy Susan in the center was bought on eBay," Kafka says. And while the lamp over the table and the dark couch in the living room are IKEA designs, and two armchairs were retrieved from someone's curb, the living room arc lamp is from Design Within Reach and a George Nelson bench used for a coffee table was bought through Herman Miller.

Despite a rather rocky start with their dream house, they don't regret the move one bit. Borsellino even sees how Eichler and his architects continued to learn what worked and what didn't as they built their numerous tracts. "Our previous Eichler was the beta plan for this later model; this house is much more functional," he says. "They had 15,000 tries to get it right and they did."

Facing: The family room and kitchen share one expansive space. The couch and light fixture are new, while the dining table, chairs, and bar cart are vintage.

Above: In this Eichler model, the living room is separate from the kitchen and family room, but still has plenty of light and architectural detailing.

Desert Alexander

When Nick Lorenzen was visiting a friend in Palm Springs, he fell in love with a neighborhood of homes built in the late '50s by the Alexander Construction Company. He ended up buying a 1,200-square-foot home a couple of blocks away with the same floor plan as his friend's.

The investment was a bit of a gamble, as the neighborhood was run down and most homes were for sale or had bars on their windows. But he was among the pioneers who saw the midcentury tract's potential, and three years later the area has undergone a renaissance. "Since I've lived here, my block has completely turned around; it's beautiful now," he says.

Structurally, the tract house was in good condition, and by refreshing the finishes and cleaning up the yard and pool, Lorenzen made the home look new again. He did much of the work himself—painting, a new fence, landscaping, removing layers of carpet and linoleum from the concrete slab before putting on a new top coat—and had pros do the big jobs: driveway replacement and a new foam roof. "I did everything on a hairdresser's budget, one project at a time over five years," he says.

The three-bedroom, two-bath house has a typical open floor plan with the kitchen, dining, and living room sharing one space. A wall of windows opens up to a shaded patio and pool via sliding glass doors. "People are always shocked that it feels so big," he notes. "I count the covered patio seating area as part of my home, too."

Lorenzen's rooms are furnished with vintage and reproduction pieces. A George Nelson couch and chair came from the home of a Herman Miller employee, and many of his tables, lamps, and decorative elements were picked up at Palm Springs-area thrift stores. His design sensibilities are secure enough to stir in a 1947 green-and-black vinyl dinette set that's a family heirloom—a piece seemingly at odds with the later modern classics. Somehow it all works against his neutral palette of white walls and scored concrete floors lit by the brilliant desert sunlight.

Facing: The guest bedroom has a bit more kitsch thrown into the mix: a Harry Bertoia-designed chair sits next to a generic Danish modern bed with an Alexander Calder-motif bedspread. The Carlo of Hollywood artwork in the asymmetrical frames is either good "bad" art or high camp—depending on your point of view.

Below: Alexander Construction, a firm that specialized in affordable second homes and doubled the size of Palm Springs in the '50s and '60s, built this 1958 ranch house.

Architect William Krisel varied the rooflines, front facades, and siting of the Palm Springs tract homes, but the floor plans are basically the same.

Way-Back **Machine**

An almost totally original ranch house built in 1966 came to the second owners with its popcorn ceilings, vintage kitchen appliances, tuck-and-roll wet bar, built-in barbecues, and monolithic S-shaped living room rock wall intact. There was original terrazzo in the entry, pristine paneling, and a bathroom with fleurs-de-lis on the shower enclosure doors.

The floor plan is a bit more traditional than post-and-beam midcentury homes: a rather dark front entry opens up to a living room with floor-to-ceiling glass overlooking a patio with views of the surrounding hillsides and downtown Los Angeles. Low-ceilinged hallways lead to bedrooms and baths on the right, while another narrow hall takes you to the combined family room/kitchen on the left. This space is the heart of the house.

"The family room had one of the coolest wet bars we'd ever seen," owner Apryl Lundsten says about their first looky-loo tour of the home. "It's upholstered in black-and-silver vinyl and has four mint-condition barstools. Next to it is an indoor barbecue with a rotisserie and all of the original tools, and above it on the rock wall is a built-in clock that still works. The place was obviously a party pad."

The adjoining kitchen, with its vintage stainless-steel built-in appliances—cooktop, wall oven, refrigerator, toaster, coffeemaker, and aluminum foil dispenser—is separated from the family room by a low breakfast bar with suspended gold chairs that would be at home in a '60s Vegas coffee shop. Outside on the flagstone patio that comprises the backyard on this steep hillside lot is another barbecue built into a massive circular dining table.

Above: This ranch has a typical plain-Jane look: a stucco and flagstone facade with small aluminum windows, an attached garage, and an aggregate path leading to a mahogany double front door.

Facing: Eclectic probably best describes the family room furnishings: a Heywood-Wakefield dining table and dog-bone chairs, vintage bar stools that are suspended from the breakfast counter, and coffee table and green sectional that came with the house. Yes, the rotary wall phone in the kitchen still works, as do the original appliances.

Apryl and husband David Spancer have left the house alone while getting to know it, and other than an engineered wood floor in the family room, the home looks much as it did when it was built. They found their eclectic collection of vintage and retro-influenced furniture fit right in.

The couple christened the house with a party that included Marisa McBride, one of three daughters of the original owners. She shared old photos and anecdotes about growing up in the house, and when she saw the orange beautician's sink in the laundry room off the kitchen, she got teary-eyed. "I have the hairdresser's chair that matches the sink," she said. "I'd love for you guys to have it. Mom would want it to be here."

Facing: The living room of this traditional ranch has an S-shaped flagstone wall, a cantilevered slate hearth, and ubiquitous popcorn ceilings.

Below: The lounge-lizard bar was what really grabbed the new owners when they first toured the house: what could be cooler than glittery vinyl barstools and tuck-and-roll upholstery?

Houston **Nights**

A small Pfister settee from Knoll, glass-topped coffee table from Scope Furniture, and B&B Italia wall storage unit furnish this Houston living room. The shoji screen was moved to the window wall, but originally closed the living room off from the dining room.

Houston's postwar houses are typically brick affairs, with styles ranging from neo-Colonial white-pillar ranches to flat-roof Modernist designs. In the Memorial Bend neighborhood, Cathie and Rick Johnson have been in their 1958 house for more than twenty years. Only the third owners, the couple inherited a largely original but neglected house with brown shag carpeting and a ferocious insect infestation.

The long, low house is almost hidden by the mature trees on the large 90-foot by 110-foot lot, and the street facade is private to the point that it might be mistaken for a library or a walled compound. Originally, the sole front windows were narrow clerestories sandwiched between the top of the brick walls and the two-foot roof overhang. A porte cochere—a drive-through, roofed shelter at the front entrance and a popular feature in Houston—hides cars from view and stands in for a garage or a carport.

The 2,300-square-foot house came to the Johnsons with an incongruous bay window on the front and a tacked-on metal structure known as a "Western Room" that took up a big chunk of the backyard and blocked light from the family room. The couple tore off the shed immediately but debated about bricking up the unoriginal bay window to restore the front facade.

"Because it let some needed sunlight into the kitchen's breakfast area and the view was nice, we decided to keep the window," Cathie, an interior designer, says. The couple lived with the bay window for years, but eventually found a more midcentury-appropriate version, an aluminum-framed casement model from RAM Industries.

There was an almost-new Wood-Mode kitchen in place when the Johnsons bought in 1983, so they kept that but recently lowered the height of the bar between the family room and kitchen and put in new limestone counters. Other than the original cooktop, appliances have been replaced, and a modern ventilating fan and improved lighting installed. The glass table and see-through wire Bertoia chairs in the small breakfast area help keep it from seeming claustrophobic.

The Johnsons have some midcentury furniture—the Bertoia chairs and a rosewood Eames lounge chair and ottoman they bought in 1981—but prefer a contemporary sensibility. Cathie upholstered the entry hall walls in a tan silk, installed a wall of smoky glass in the guest bath to go with its original black terrazzo, and annexed closet space to expand the master bath to include a Jacuzzi tub.

She also designed a horizontal-slat wood fence along the side of the property that mimics the bands of brick across the front facade. It helps disguise the presence of a highway that cut through Memorial Bend about ten years ago. In the backyard, another decorative grid fence backed by window screening camouflages a storage shed.

Like the Johnsons, the house and the neighborhood have evolved in the past twenty years. "People don't always realize how comfortable modern architecture is," Cathie says. "We bought a home with good bones; it just needed a little TLC."

Left: The sturdy rustic chopping block gives the kitchen a shot of personality. The glass hood of the exhaust fan helps keep the breakfast nook part of the kitchen and blocks a minimum of light from the new aluminum windows.

Above: The entry to this Houston home, set back between the lanterns, is hidden from the street. The semicircular driveway passes through a porte cochere, which stands in for a garage or carport.

Appreciating **the Intent**

A 1955 custom home with
Googie-esque lines has
quite an impact as you
approach up a steep
private drive.

Only the second owner of a 1955 home designed by Southern California architect Clair Earl, Chris Burusco realized he'd stumbled across a gem when his realtor drove him up the steep private driveway to the home. "I knew I wanted a '50s modern house—one with a flat roof, glass walls, a carport in front," he says, "and it took about six months of looking to find one. Most were 1970s stucco boxes or '50s ranch houses without all the bells and whistles I wanted. This one was a diamond in the rough."

He gently took the house back to what it was meant to be, which pleased the 93-year-old seller no end. Jean Russom and her late husband, Alan Dailey, built the home, which had a Palos Verdes stone fireplace and chimney, polished concrete floors throughout, radiant heating in the living room and patio floors, vibrant colors for each of the sliding doors in the kitchen and carport cabinets, and a built-in stereo speaker in the hallway to the bedrooms.

Alan died only months after the couple moved in, and during the years that followed, an interior decorator friend of Russom's took over and made sweeping changes that included draperies on the floor-to-ceiling windows, wallpaper, and other modifications not in keeping with the original intent. "The decorator did everything opposite to what was done in the first place and I was in no emotional condition to argue," she says. "My talents lay in other directions, I guess, and it got into a mess. I'm so glad that it's put back to where it should be now."

the house is so **different from anything**
I ever thought **of doing,** *but* **its wonderful.** *I just can't* **imagine doing it any better.**

The 1,950-square-foot house has three bedrooms and two baths. An angular living room with a pass-through bar to the compact kitchen and dining area is the most dynamic space, with its channeled wood ceiling and prow-like white wall and soffit.

Burusco had wall-to-wall carpet taken up, the concrete slab sealed, and cork squares put down that look as if they are original. The project was fiscally daunting, though. "The first bid was for $24,000 from a local flooring company," he remembers. "But a tile guy who had worked on a local showcase house said he'd do it for about a third of that." Except for the original slate floor in the entryway and the tiled baths, there is now cork throughout the house.

Coming from a condo with roommates, Burusco didn't have much in the way of midcentury furnishings. He did own a tan leather Eames lounge chair and ottoman, a couple of Danish modern pieces, and four Eames DAR shell chairs with original bases. Joining them are a new Warren Platner–designed coffee table in the living room and an affordable Modernica Case Study series couch, both lit by a "Polluce" floor lamp from Artemide. A vintage Jens Risom armchair with orange cushions is a particular favorite, as is his Saarinen dining table, which bears the dings of a previous owner's daily use.

"The house is so different from anything I ever thought of doing, but it's wonderful. I just can't imagine doing it any better," Russom says. "The fact that Chris loves the house—that's the most important thing of all."

Facing: The living room is all angles and interesting surfaces: the cork floor isn't original but is typical of the period, and the ceiling and far wall are tongue-and-groove solid wood. The entire room is lit by a wall of floor-to-ceiling windows and slid-ing glass doors, which lead out to the covered patio and view of the foothills.

Above: This small area in the kitchen stands in for a dining room in the custom-designed house. With a large window looking out toward the front driveway on the south, a sliding glass door leading to a small patio to the west, and a pass-through to the living room on the north wall, the diminutive space doesn't feel tight.

As Original **as it Gets**

The gable-roof atrium models are some of the most arresting Eichler designs. The area to the right of the front door functions as a carport, plus there is an attached two-car garage. Behind the orange door is the private atrium, which adds additional living space to the floor plan.

As much as they love the architecture of their A. Quincy Jones–designed Eichler, Clay and Cindy Morrow are really there for the neighborhood. With the advent of their first child, the couple decided they needed to move somewhere safer with better parking, more level streets, good schools, a larger single-level house—in short, a family neighborhood. When plans to build a prefab house fizzled, their friends were aghast to learn they were considering moving an hour away to outer suburbia. And move they did.

There are about 125 homes built by Joseph Eichler in Thousand Oaks, California. The Morrows' five-bedroom house dates from 1964, and they bought it from the original owner. Other than needing cleaning and painting, the house was relatively unscathed. "We knew that it was potentially great because it had almost no '70s remodeling done to it. That was a huge plus," Cindy says.

The Morrows note the Japanese architectural influences seen in their home, particularly the aggregate entry floor in the living room. "It's normally the first thing to go when people remodel these homes," Cindy comments. "My grandfather's house in Japan had an aggregate floor where you'd take off your shoes before entering the home. It's a subtle transition to the inside."

Their biggest project turned out to be removing the damaged original tile under the wall-to-wall carpeting. Neither wood nor carpet over the radiant heating made sense to them, and the slab had cracks and stains once Cindy finished removing the tile adhesive with solvent. (The couple vetoed the idea of sanding off the adhesive due to concerns about airborne asbestos.) They decided to have a new self-leveling 1/8-inch-thick cement coating poured over the existing slab, which ran about half the price of wood flooring.

Below: The living room has floor-to-ceiling views of the backyard on both sides of the brick fireplace. The Danish modern chairs and side table are paired with a new couch and a vintage Oriental rug.

Facing: This Eichler's kitchen is just about original, including the low cooking peninsula and swing-out table that offers convenient seating for the family's children.

"I like the fact that we don't have everything by a designer, either vintage or reissued, and I like that our furniture is a mix of different eras," Cindy continues. "We might have a modern couch, but it's sitting next to a Scandinavian side chair or a table from 1940 with an inlaid tile top. If we like something, we get it; it doesn't matter who made it or where it came from."

EICHLER'S REACH

Joseph Eichler became a builder in the late '40s, when housing for some 10 million veterans, many of whom were starting families, was a major driving force in the economy. The homes' post-and-beam construction allowed for open floor plans and walls of glass facing private backyards, and incorporated such innovations as radiant floor heating. Eichler's willingness to hire talented architects and his devotion to quality craftsmanship and modern living resulted in houses that looked custom but were within reach of first-time homebuyers.

Almost all Eichlers are in California—350 homes in Orange, 200-plus more in Thousand Oaks and Granada Hills, 60 or so in Sacramento, and in the San Francisco Bay Area, several thousand more, including two tracts that are now on the National Register of Historic Places. Four years ago, the Society of Architectural Historians held a hugely popular tour of Orange County Eichlers, and today the homes are greatly prized.

"The floor was kind of a disaster," Clay concedes. "We had to stain it darker than we wanted, the texture is different from room to room because the people who did it didn't have experience with this particular product, and it shows every pet hair."

Almost all their furnishings were purchased inexpensively from thrift stores or eBay, or are hand-me-downs. A couch in the family room and the Persian rug in the living room are the only things they purchased for this home.

"We're not fans of houses that don't look lived in," Cindy says, "with all that perfect, expensive furniture. Clay and I both feel that there's too much good design to only have things that are from 1964."

"Just going to a store and buying a living room or bedroom of reissued furniture doesn't have the right feeling," Clay adds. "That seems forced and impersonal."

Colorado Modernism

A Bertoia Bird chair and ottoman pick up the colors in the artwork over the fireplace in this Colorado home. A $20 Eames plywood dish table with "issues," according to the owners, holds a Bennington elephant and a lion by Lisa Larson for Gustavsberg. The pole lamp is by Lightolier, and two George Nelson vintage clocks hang on the wall next to an Eames leg splint.

Frank Sarcia and Jim Eveleth have been collecting modern furniture for fifteen years. When they found a '50s house in Arapaho Hills in the Denver suburb of Littleton, it all gelled: this was the home they and their furniture were meant to have.

"The house wasn't run down really," Sarcia says, "but it needed paint badly and the wood was in poor condition in some places. The previous owners were in their eighties and thank God nothing had been changed. It still had the original range and oven, vintage bathroom cabinets, and original wall sconces. That's really what I was looking for in a house."

The pair kept their midcentury galley kitchen with its original sliding-door cabinets, and painted the architectural elements in Mondrian-esque hues—bright orange, green, and white. The pony wall separating their living room from the kitchen was painted yellow, in marked contrast with the new slate floors, gray cement block fireplace wall, and dark tongue-and-groove wood ceiling.

Their living room is a veritable midcentury museum. A vintage Eames sofa and surfboard table, reissued Harry Bertoia Bird chair and ottoman, and a George Nelson Coconut chair with original fabric are iconic pieces. One of their favorite sources is Mod Livin' in Denver, but they're also inveterate yard-salers. Even their den and kitchen are packed with modern stuff: Catherine Holmes bowls atop the kitchen cabinets, and an

early Womb chair and Evans-label Eames plywood chair flank the TV.

The home was built by Clyde Mannon, who worked on nearby Arapahoe Acres as well. Sarcia and Eveleth's house has transom windows among the fixed clerestories, and the decorative block detailing seen on the fireplace wall is repeated on the front facade and on the garage wall. A quirk of the house is the two entry doors: the left one leads to the front hall and living room, while the right-hand one provides access to the furnace.

Above: Arapaho Hills near Denver is the location of this '50s tract home.

Right: The mosaic ceramic tile in this original bath is back in style, while the angle-front vanity packs as much storage as possible into the compact space.

Facing: Saarinen dining chairs from Mod Livin' in Denver surround a matching table in the kitchen's dining nook; over them hangs a Nelson saucer lamp. In the adjoining living room, a Nelson Coconut chair dates from 1957.

the living room is a veritable midcentury museum *a* vintage Eames sofa, *reissued* Harry Bertoia Bird chair *and ottoman,* *and a* George Nelson Coconut chair *with original fabric.*

Is My House a Ranch?

The postwar ranch house
has many moods: wild
Modernist, safe traditionalist,
split-level suburbanite,
unassuming stucco box. And
local custom may slap other
names on the variable style:
rancher, traditional, rambler,
contemporary, raised ranch,
and most often, "starter
home."

Hallmarks of the **Style**

Above: One of Denver's many traditional ranch homes.

Facing: Cliff May houses have patios reached via wood-frame french doors.

If you ask someone what type of home he or she has, often they pause, seemingly at a loss. "I don't know; it doesn't really have a style," they might say. Chances are the ubiquitous "just a house" is a ranch. When one home might be a wild Googie-inspired '60s interpretation of modern with an outlandish raked roof, and another a prim schoolmarm of a house, all polite brick and sober clapboard, it can be hard to see they shared the same drawing board.

But it's the details that matter and that make the ranch such a residential success story: the walls of glass, fanciful rooflines, open floor plans, atriums, post-and-beam construction, quiet facades, clerestory windows, and more.

HISTORY

The ranch house has its roots in the mid-nineteenth-century adobe ranchos of the West. These homes were themselves based on architectural forms from Spain and Mexico, and borrowed from the California missions as well. Often L- or U-shaped with a covered veranda or "corredor" skirting a central patio, the front facade was usually plain, while the back elevation had rooms that opened to the porch or the patio. Sound familiar?

Cliff May, a Southern California builder who is often credited with fathering the proliferation of the style, began designing small ranch houses in the '30s. He would go on to craft both impressive custom ranches of 6,000 square feet as well as tracts of partially prefabbed two-bedroom homes under 1,000 square feet.

But it was the postwar need for lots of houses *now* that really pushed the ranch house model into prominence. The flood of returning GIs made the quickly built, affordable modern ranch the house best suited for the optimistic future. By the end of the war, an estimated three million U.S. families needed homes; 13 million GIs only swelled those ranks further. Restrictions on building materials were lifted, and extended families that had doubled or tripled up on quarters during the Depression and the war now wanted their own piece of the American Dream. The GI Bill of Rights helped make that a reality.

Tract after tract of both Modernist and traditional ranches were built all across the nation, from Levittown in New York to Daly City in California and everywhere in between. Whether the homes made you think space-age futurism or conservative traditional values, they became hugely popular and blanketed the countryside. There were even all-steel, porcelain-clad prefab ranches called Lustrons that were trucked to sites as numbered parts, much like the kit houses that had been so popular during the preceding decades. In 1950 alone, 1.5 million homes were built, most of them ranches. By the late '50s and early '60s it was hard to remember when ranch homes weren't the American housing standard.

Although the architecture can vary significantly—a split-level '60s rambler versus a long, low Eichler or Midwestern brick ranch—these postwar homes have distinctive features in common.

Above: Traditional ranches such as this one in Arcadia, California, proved popular with wealthier buyers.

Left: Daly City near San Francisco.

Facing: Buyers flocked to postwar ranch house tracts like this one near Denver.

Better Homes
and Gardens
1958
IDEA HOME
featuring famous products
advertised in
Better Homes & Gardens

AUG. 24 thru SEPT. 7

MANNON ASSOCIATES INC.

ROOFLINES

The sometimes whimsical roofs are the first thing many people notice. Flat, butterfly, steeply pitched, saw-tooth, and a dozen variations on these themes are commonly seen, particularly in homes that were designed to appeal to modern sensibilities. Other more traditional styles have hip roofs based on early 1900s Prairie School architecture, or the ubiquitous side-gable roof that seems to be the most popular design of all.

FRONT FACADES

"Private" best describes the street visage of most ranch homes. While they can seem a tad boring when it comes to curb appeal, the front facades display a whole range of materials: stucco, board and batten, brick, stone veneer, vertical or horizontal wood siding, cement block, clapboard, and more. Perforated block privacy walls, exaggerated eaves, decorative shutters, and fanciful dovecotes are other common touches.

OPEN FLOOR PLANS

The merged-function room of the ranch house was a modern departure from compartmentalized living. While bedrooms and baths could most often be found in a wing with a central hall, the public spaces for entertaining, dining, cooking, and relaxing became one. Larger ranches tended to place this public area in the center of the home, separating children's bedrooms from the adult wing, perhaps the beginning of today's trend for master suites. These floor plans can be simple boxes or rectangles, or have more rambling U- or L-shapes. On tighter lots, the split-level rambler with a garage tucked under the living space and a daylight basement was a popular solution.

1. A butterfly roof split-level ranch near San Francisco.

2. An A-frame roofline in Denver.

3. A hip-roof stucco box in Westchester, California.

4. Split-level ranches were built on sloping or narrow lots.

5. One of Houston's modern flat-roof ranches.

6. In Denver, this dining room, kitchen, and living room all flow together.

7. A Cliff May home has had the partition wall between the kitchen and living room removed to open it up fully.

WINDOWS & WALLS OF GLASS

Step inside the front door of a ranch, and the surprise is the expansive view through the rear wall of glass. Not every postwar home has this heavy emphasis on bringing the outside in, but light and plenty of it is what sets the midcentury ranch apart from its predecessors. Architects achieved this through floor-to-ceiling windows, sliding glass doors and clerestories—windows that go up right to the roofline. In more traditional ranches, you'll see bay, diamond-paned, and double-hung windows as well.

POST AND BEAM & "PONY" WALLS

Typical midcentury construction consisted of posts that supported beams, which in turn carried the roof load, allowing for both exterior walls of glass and non-load-bearing interior walls. Because of this, when Modernist ranch houses did have walls dividing the public space, they often stopped short of the ceiling—pony walls—or had large pass-throughs. This kept even a partially enclosed kitchen more open and allowed it to share light with adjoining rooms—an internal window, in effect.

ATRIUMS & PATIOS

Nothing said indoor-outdoor like ranches that included entry atriums— an open-air patio between the entry door and the interior itself. Typically two or three rooms open directly into these private areas via sliding glass or french doors, making the differentiation between yard and house a moot point in temperate climates. For homes without atriums, rear or side patios served a similar function and helped modest-size houses live larger than their square footage would suggest.

1. Brick fireplaces were often juxtaposed with large panes of glass.

2. When the sliding glass doors are open, the patio and family room are virtually one.

3. A clerestory window.

4. Post-and-beam construction was used in both the house and its carport.

5. The kitchen is screened off from the dining and family room space, while a pass-through makes it convenient for the cook.

6. Non-load-bearing pony walls divide midcentury floor plans without blocking daylight from the interior rooms.

7. A contorted ficus tree grows in the atrium of a Thousand Oaks, California, Eichler.

8. A once-rural ranch house has both front and rear patios.

CARPORTS & GARAGES

Postwar, the automobile allowed the population to spread out into the newly minted suburbs, and its hold on American life was evident in the pride-of-place location of the attached garage or carport. Some designs, like Joseph Eichler's California homes, nearly brought the family car into the house. More traditional styles still had a detached garage at the back of the property, or on tight or sloping lots, under the house next to the entry stairs.

INTERIORS

Ranch interiors varied as much as their exteriors. Baths and kitchens were compact and traditional immediately postwar, employing many of the same appliances and fixture styles used in the '30s and early '40s. But by the '60s, contemporary design had made huge inroads, and sliding kitchen cabinet doors, conversation pits, and streamlined, modern surfaces signaled this was not your momma's house.

TRADITION MEETS MODERN: MATERIALS

Midcentury houses still emphasized time-honored materials: flagstone, brick, wood, tile, plaster, terrazzo, grass cloth, cork, and linoleum. But modern materials like aluminum and steel windows, Formica counters, drywall, plywood cabinetry, electric kitchens, and aggregate floors joined newer building techniques—cement slab foundations, radiant heating, and tar-and-gravel roofs—to make the postwar ranch house a mix of old and new technology.

1. Like Eichlers, this Portland, Oregon, Rummer has both a front carport and an attached garage.

2. This dramatic carport extends the eaves of a midcentury ranch in Denver.

3. Detached garages at the rear of the lot were still popular postwar, like this cement block double garage.

4. A model home in Littleton, Colorado, displayed the latest in contemporary furnishings and streamlined kitchen surfaces.

5. This brochure for an all-steel Lustron home emphasized the compact efficiency of the smaller postwar home.

6. Aggregate flooring, grass cloth, and mahogany paneling.

7. Scored and polished cement.

3

2

4

THE KITCHEN - Right side view. Additional storage cabinets, exhaust fan and combination automatic dish washer-clothes washer built right into the sink. Stove and refrigerator are not included, but standard makes fit floor space.

THE KITCHEN—Left side view. Note the convenient "pass through" to the dining area; the big work counter and the built-in cabinets with sliding doors. And how easy a porcelain enamel kitchen is to keep clean!

6

7

Stunning Transformations

Take a look at these amazing ranch houses with a new lease on life, thanks to recent remodels by forward-thinking owners. Fresh finishes, improved floor plans, innovative solutions, and modest additions that live large: real-world renovations with real budgets.

Cheap **Thrills**

Toni and Mark Galloro, the parents of three children between the ages of eight and fifteen, bought their Cliff May ranch home in 1988. "Our house was the gathering place for the neighborhood—it wasn't unusual for ten kids at a time to be running in and out—so we just gave up and decided not to stress over any damage," Toni says. "We never quite got it right before," Mark, who works in construction, adds about their interior. They decided to enlist pros this time.

Now it's quite a different house. Working with architects Patrick Killen and Christian Navar of STUDIO 9 ONE 2, the couple traded an awkward kitchen and choppy layout for a bold modern interior. From a contemporary kitchen with a frosted window backsplash, to affordable modern furniture and a concrete-block dividing wall separating an entry from the living room, the Galloros have embraced something bold for their second fifteen years.

The new location for the kitchen is the former family room, which was one step down from the rest of the floor plan; it has a polished cement floor with terrazzo-like tile inserts. The attached garage was turned into a kid-friendly media room, and the family now has a real space for their dining table, which looks out through bifold doors to a small patio. With the Nana doors stacked off to the side, the indoors and out function as one—or the glass-and-metal table can be moved right outside when mood dictates.

"We wanted to be respectful of the original architecture and do something in the vein of what Cliff May might do today," Killen says. "We pushed the kitchen out to the front of the house and used the glass backsplash to create interest on the front

we pushed the kitchen out **to the front of the house** *and used the glass* **backsplash to create** **interest** *on the front of* **the building.**

Facing: In the dining area, folding doors stack flat to the wall, opening up this Cliff May house to its side patio.

Above: In the before shot, the T-shaped kitchen was behind the orange wall. Now this same area is a defined entry hall, and a new cement block wall separates it from the living room.

of the building. One of the difficulties with tract housing and houses on small lots is contending with the garage door on the front of the building."

"Our goal was to use our craft to insert an added functionality in an attempt to enhance the lives of our clients and how they use the space," adds Navar. "The hope is that in the end you're successful and your design adds to May's timelessness. The last thing you ever want—and even fear—is that the next family and their architect that drive through looking for inspiration in the neighborhood, see your design and say, 'Wow! Who butchered that house?' "

Mark and Toni were able to use some higher-end finishes than their budget would normally have allowed since Mark works in the trade, but that doesn't mean he's immune to missteps. The ceiling of their ranch is wide tongue-and-groove boards with beams every six feet. In the kitchen area he installed drywall and can lights in between the beams. It wasn't until he was done that he realized that idea was a mistake: the room just didn't seem right without its trademark post-and-beam ceiling. So he ripped out the drywall and repainted to emphasize the architecture—to great effect.

During the remodel, the front door was relocated from its spot next to the fireplace, and a new entry hall

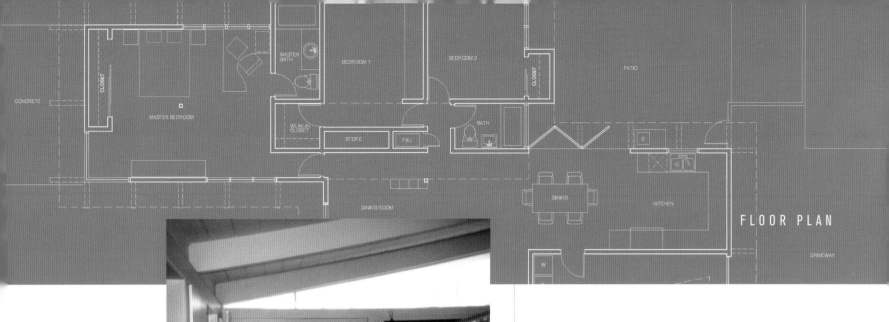

FLOOR PLAN

Facing: The custom kitchen cabinets are Douglas fir with a Mondrian-inspired detail that repeats in the entry storage unit and on an accent wall near the dining table.

Right: Neither functional nor original, the former kitchen had little to recommend its preservation.

was equipped with built-ins that handle incoming clutter: shoe cubbies are designed as art, and backpack and sports equipment storage is behind doors. The Galloros' sons share a bedroom, so the architects worked to expand it slightly by borrowing closet space from their sister's room. Her replacement closet bumps out into the patio and is the only added square footage; by cladding it in metal, the appendage draws your eye and looks interesting instead of being a tacked-on eyesore.

The burnished cement block used in the entry wall was a special order but still a standard building material. "It's a fairly inexpensive material, yet elegant because it's honed like stone," Killen says, "and the lights are simple wall sockets behind Plexiglas. They're what I call cheap thrills. Great projects start with great clients, not necessarily great budgets. People who are willing to be very innovative mean you don't have to spend $500 a square foot to build a really fun building."

Architect of **Their Future**

Above: This Houston ranch has a double hip roof, brick facade, and its original aluminum casement windows. The homeowners installed a reflective-foil radiant barrier inside the attic and insulated all of the walls.

Facing: The living room has modern icons wherever you look: the chrome-leg chairs and the ottomans in the corner are from Minotti, the cardboard side table was designed by Frank Gehry in the '70s, and the coffee table is an Isamu Noguchi reissue. An Eames Time Life Building walnut stool sits under a charcoal by local artist Bob Russell, and Aaron Parazette did the large painting over the B&B Italia daybed. The shag area rug is stain-resistant wall-to-wall carpeting cut and bound for $500. In the dining room, bentwood chairs designed by Gehry surround a B&B Italia table that seats 14 in the small room. A reissued Jens Risom chair is in the corner.

Desperate enough to bid on a house sight unseen in Houston's hot real estate market, Karen Lantz and Andy Farkas actually did pretty well buying their pig-in-a-poke. There turned out to be slow leaks in the two baths, and the home was dirty and in need of renovation after years as a rental, but Lantz, who was in architecture school at the time, saw its attributes.

"These houses were well built compared to today's standards, so other than foundation or sewage problems, there's not a lot that can be wrong," she says. "They used tighter grain, more dimensionally stable lumber, and the ceramic tile was installed with metal lath and one-inch to two-inch mortar beds."

Those leaking pipes led to complete remodels of the baths in the 1954 house, and the kitchen soon followed suit. Lantz believes in keeping the architectural envelope intact and the interior in scale, but considers homes like theirs nondescript in a lot of ways. The couple opted for a thoroughly modern rendition of midcentury. While they may have iconic furniture designed fifty years ago, and a growing collection of original art, contemporary makers like B&B Italia, Minotti, and Droog are welcome.

Budget was a consideration for the young couple, and they scrimped on some elements while splurging on others. In the kitchen, which was demolished back to the studs, affordable stock cabinets from Home Depot have granite counters. The appliances are Frigidaire "Gallery Series" models bought off the showroom floor, and their prep/snack table is from Pottery Barn. But then there's the Dornbracht faucet, Knoll Jamaica barstools, and Droog milk-bottle pendant lamps that let you know the occupants care greatly about good design.

In the baths, trendy mosaic glass tile lines the walls, and scrap travertine marble tops more Home Depot cabinets. The bath in the master bedroom is particularly tiny, so Lantz chose to separate the toilet and sink from the shower with a low wall and a ceiling-mounted shower curtain that hangs from the same hardware hospitals use for privacy curtains. The Italian-looking sconces are $9.95 models from IKEA, and in the guest bath, the vanity lights are simple porcelain sockets from the hardware store with half-silvered bare bulbs.

As beautiful as their home and furnishings are now, Lantz and Farkas didn't neglect the basics. Due to soil movement, the plumbing connections had failed, so they replumbed with PVC. To help with the hot Houston summers, they put a radiant shield in the attic and insulated all of the walls before installing new drywall.

Lantz feels strongly that hiring an architect for a major renovation or remodel is key. "You can't see, feel or touch what an architect brings to a project. It's not tangible. But they offer logic of process and experience, and they are the homeowner's advocate to help them speak the construction language," she says.

Equally important in her view is hiring the right general contractor. "It's too hard for a homeowner to do their normal job everyday and try to be the general contractor, too. It's usually a disaster."

A case in point might be the couple's own experience with getting their hardwood floors repaired and refinished. The first pro they found did a poor job—sanding marks and hair left in the high-gloss finish. Lantz figured she and her husband could do a better job during a break from school, but as it turned out, not by much. They then hired a second company to fix what they had personally wrought. Still unhappy with the results, they hired the most expensive and reputedly best floor company in town, who insisted the homeowners move out for the two-week process.

"That was a great lesson about getting what you pay for and about quality control," she says. "There were painful construction lessons learned on this house that make me more valuable to my clients today."

Clean **Slate**

The view from the entry atrium of the Orange, California, home.

Todd and Mindy Hatch knew right away that they wanted to knock down some walls and remove the worn kitchen and mahogany paneling in their 1962 Eichler in Orange, California. They bought the 2,100-square-foot post-and-beam house in 2003 and spent the first three months living elsewhere while they gutted and began to rebuild much of the interior. They removed a wall that divided the kitchen and family room from the living and dining space in order to create the wide-open floor plan Todd envisioned for the house.

"We definitely didn't want the division between the two areas. Like us, most people spend a lot of their time in the kitchen and the family room, and we wanted to enjoy the whole house and the indoor/outdoor feel of looking out to the backyard," he says.

When the Hatches moved in, it was with a makeshift kitchen and a child who was beginning to crawl. "Buying an old home is like opening a can of worms: there's always a problem with something and things take longer than you think," Mindy says philosophically.

Todd, a restaurant designer, knew what he wanted for the new kitchen and did much of the installation himself. "The best modern designs are from the Italian companies; ours is a more modest-priced Italian kitchen," he says. Some of the cherrywood Cesar cabinets had to be customized on site to fit American appliances. "European cabinets aren't sized for a 36-inch oven—they fit something like a little Gaggenau," Todd explains.

Facing and below right: Although still largely original, the homeowners found the kitchen to be too small, dark, and cutoff from the rest of the house to suit them. In addition to the full wall between the kitchen and dining room, there was a partition wall dividing the family room and kitchen, seen here in the before shot.

Below: Thanks to the post-and-beam construction, the dining, living, and family rooms are now completely open to the kitchen.

The countertops are stainless steel, as are the appliances—an Amana refrigerator, a Marvel under-counter fridge for kid-accessible drinks, and Dacor for the cooktop, pop-up ventilating fan, oven, and microwave. Eichlers originally had small 30-inch-high breakfast tables at the end of the kitchen islands. The Hatches wanted to keep that feature, but raised it to a 36-inch height and use Bertoia counter stools for quick meals. The two islands that make up the open galley kitchen are wrapped in travertine marble and cherry veneer that matches the cabinetry; the backsplash is marble as well. The couple spent about $25,000 on the kitchen, but estimate it would likely have run $45,000–$50,000 if contracted out.

Todd wanted terrazzo throughout the whole house, but Mindy lobbied for the warmth of wood. They went with dark-stained walnut veneer flooring in the living and dining areas, and in their master bedroom and bath. Terrazzo was installed in the kitchen and family room, then along the front entry wall of windows and down the hall

to the other bedrooms and second bath. "Terrazzo went so well with the style of the house," Todd comments. "It's current but complements midcentury modern. It looked great fifty years ago and looks great today."

The fireplace and chimney were painted when they bought the house. Todd wanted to bring it back to the natural cement block color, so he had a sandblaster come out. "I just wanted him to take off the paint and leave it as smooth as possible, but it started to pit the concrete and we weren't able to get the paint out of all the nooks and crannies," he says. "It turned out way too rough. A good compromise was a hard trowel-plaster finish that kept the original joint lines."

Next on the docket for their modern ranch is storage units for the family room and doing something—they don't know what yet—with the pool-dominated backyard. Mindy eyes some nearby remodels with interest, such as neighbors who are expanding their bedroom wing six feet into the 10-foot side yard—she'd love to have a larger bathroom and more closet space she says. Odds are, the Hatches will cook up an equally ambitious plan for their bedrooms and baths.

Left: The living room has Eichler-orange siding that runs from the front atrium to the back window over-looking the pool. The homeowner designed the couch—which he likens to a low, deep Minotti knock-off—and nesting coffee tables made of Macassar ebony and zebrawood with a high-gloss finish and chrome legs. A white bench from B&B Italia and a shag area rug pull it together.

Above: In this before view, the old L-shaped kitchen wall wrapped around two posts that are now exposed. The couch sits roughly in the same spot as today's version.

Kitchen **Magicians**

Above: The old kitchen had just a few elements worth saving, including the birch upper cabinets.

Facing: After the renovation, the same kitchen balances industrial appliances and cement counters and floors with painted and stained wood.

It's said that kitchens are the most remodeled room in the house and it can be hard to resist falling for what's currently popular: stainless steel appliances, granite counters, and wood cabinetry floor to ceiling. But avocado and copper-tone fridges, Formica counters, and vinyl floors were hot sellers in their day, and it's only in retrospect that a style looks laughable or dated—and not in a good way.

Much of a kitchen's style longevity depends upon making choices appropriate to the architecture—no home-improvement-center specials in a Victorian or country kitchens in a modern ranch. These examples do include some of today's current trends, but the home-owners have worked to integrate the cooking areas into the overall aesthetics of their open floor plans, and in some cases have gone back to decidedly midcentury cues.

Kevin Cwayna's 1954 ranch still had original birch plywood cabinets on the end wall, but an awkward-height divider had been added to the counter separating the living area from the kitchen. The counters were '70s white tile and the lower cabinets had seen better days.

Cwayna gutted most of the room, had new cabinetry built to coordinate with the original, and personally fabricated 4-inch-thick concrete counters for the T-shaped workspace. Moonstone and green pebble aggregate was added to the top layer and the surface was polished with a diamond sander. The existing cement slab floor was scored in a 32-inch grid and polished as well. "I love the island because it looks like it's sculpted from the floor and really fits in a heavy post-and-beam house," he says.

Cwayna shopped for equally heavy-duty appliances, including industrial faucets used in hospitals, a restaurant-quality icemaker, a commercial Traulsen fridge and DCS

stove, a drinking fountain that dispenses filtered water, and two stainless steel sinks. A Bosch dishwasher is the only residential-grade appliance.

Elsewhere in his neighborhood, Lisa and Rob Steele took a house that has a flopped floor plan from Cwayna's and went contemporary. Their inherited kitchen was choppy and the cupboards were falling apart. They discussed refacing the cabinet fronts, but decided that would be pouring good money down a large hole.

Instead, the Steeles went all out and moved the water heater outdoors and the sink to the window wall. The refrigerator moved as well, and the six ungrounded electrical circuits that served the whole house were replaced with twelve grounded circuits just for the new kitchen alone. They chose granite countertops, GE Profile appliances, and maple cabinetry from Frontier Cabinets—ordering the cupboards without glass or hardware, both of which they purchased separately. Black handmade tile from Expo was chosen for the backsplash, and simple hanging pendant lights in hard-to-find black over the island contrast with the blond engineered-wood flooring.

"It took more time and energy, but we got just what we wanted," Lisa says about not going with the standard cabinetry options. "We didn't want to settle for less than we think the house deserves."

Doing something architecturally appropriate to their home drove Jon and Gayle Jarrett's kitchen renovation as well. They tracked down the blueprints of their 1960s Eichler to help envision what it once was and embraced period details.

The original kitchen had been replaced with a big-box special—raised-panel oak cabinets, brass pulls, and faux-brick vinyl flooring. They recycled the existing cupboards to

buyers who thought the style was just grand and gutted the room entirely. Inspiration for their new galley kitchen was based on the prototypical steel Eichler X-100 kitchen and their Anshen and Allen blueprints, which gave dimensions, appliance locations, and countertop heights.

"Getting the kitchen back was really pivotal to the feel of the house," Jon says. "The kitchen is the epicenter—it's where a lot of social activity takes place. I wanted Formica countertops and cabinets, that whole midcentury look."

The couple selected affordable Frigidaire appliances, including a cooktop with coils instead of hidden heating elements, which complemented the vintage look of the countertops; an 18-inch Frigidaire dishwasher was just the right size for the tight space next to the pantry.

Jon machined the round cabinet finger-hole pulls slightly larger than the standard ones you can buy because "they have more pop," and the toe kick is edged in a matching aluminum-look veneer. The pulls are sort of a visual joke, as the cabinet doors don't actually slide but spring open to the touch on hidden hinges. The side of the peninsula that faces the multipurpose room mixes Formica with grass cloth inserts for visual interest.

The one thing that they eliminated was the pivoting table that would have been on the end of the cooktop peninsula. "Jon designed both a metal-top version and a Formica-top table in our plans, but at the last minute we didn't put it in because we felt it would close off the kitchen too much," Gayle explains. Instead they use a Saarinen tulip table and chairs in the adjoining family room.

Above: The mosaic tile backsplash picks up the green in the new Formica-faced cabinets.

Right: While laminate, mosaic tile, and grass cloth were used in this kitchen re-created from the original Eichler specs, it's still decidedly modern looking.

Mile-High **Makeover**

The kitchen footprint and layout were kept in this budget-driven renovation, but the designer's hand is seen in the details.

"There was a lot of pink and a lot of oak," Dean Hight comments dryly about the interior of his 1957 brick tract home in Littleton, Colorado, when he first walked through. It had been countrified with fake vines and lots of baskets, and the sellers were clearly not in love with its Modernist lines. "There wasn't a lot of the original interior finishes left, but the general bones were nice."

The split-level house had already undergone a conversion in 1960, when the carport was converted to a den, a garage was built at the back of the lot, and a side patio was enclosed to form a dining room. This bumped the original 1,800 square feet up to 2,600, but Dean, a residential designer, wanted to take it further still. After being in the house for nine years, his artist wife, Lisa Fournier, wished for an on-site studio where she could produce her portraits and other commissions. But the challenge was where to squeeze that in, along with the large woodworking shop Dean needed to produce custom furniture, and still be able to house two cars. The only way to go was up.

Fournier sometimes works on large canvases, and Hight had to be able to maneuver an eight-foot sheet of plywood in his shop, so he sunk the addition into the ground a bit to minimize its height. Stairs at the end of the dining room lead up to the north-light atelier, and a door nearby opens to the garage/workshop. The new space brings the square footage to 3,300.

The four-bedroom, two-bath home already had a multilevel floor plan, with the living room, kitchen, and dining core on one level, the family room a couple of steps down, and the bedrooms a short flight of stairs either up or down from the front entry. The new

Above: The post behind the vintage chair marks where the home originally ended. The dining room was a patio and the carpeted stairs on the left lead to the den, formerly an open carport. These changes were made just a few years after the home was built and are typical add-ons for ranch homes. The dining room built-ins and double-paned window wall are part of the recent remodel.

Right: The orange wall marks the entry to the homeowners' upstairs studio and garage/workshop. The painting of Carlos Santa is by Dean Hight, while the other two canvases are by Lisa Fournier.

Below: This Denver-area home was built with a two-story section that steps down its sloped lot. The brick-facade portion houses the bedrooms and baths, and the single-story contains the living and dining rooms, the kitchen, and a den. The designer-homeowner has added his own touches to the exterior: Frank Lloyd Wright–inspired relief panels near the flag, and a copper-painted handrail on the porch that incorporates a mailbox. The two-story addition at the rear is hidden from this vantage.

The home's new garage and two-story addition houses cars plus a woodworking shop and an artist's studio. The garage has a faux-copper door, vertical-groove and corrugated metal siding, and metal channeling emphasizing the horizontal siding on the house.

studio/shop/garage extends the L-shaped house, but by placing it at the rear of the lot, the front facade looks just the same—or maybe better with the interesting details Hight has added.

Before the latest addition, the couple did an affordable revamp of their inherited almond-laminate kitchen. They kept the existing cabinet boxes and glides, but designed new doors and installed concrete counters, which have decorative coins set into the surface. Hight considers the kitchen to have elements of "wabi sabi," which in this case he translates as "modern, clean-lined Japanese design with a touch of imperfection."

His hand is evident on almost every surface of the house, from the birch slab interior doors with painted copper detailing and the dining room's vibrant orange wall, to the metal channeling on the siding next to the garage and the Frank Lloyd Wright–inspired relief panels on the home's exterior. It turns out that Wright's Usonian houses were a big influence for Hight.

"This house was born out of that 1930s Usonian period," he says. "A lot of the Wright houses are in suburban neighborhoods or were out in natural settings that required a car; Usonians were his concept of the ideal home for the United States middle class. Stylistically they have low-slung or flat roofs, walls of glass, natural materials. They didn't look anything like the tract houses of the '30s."

The couple was living in a Victorian in Denver, but fell hard for midcentury when they toured a modern home Fournier's brother was redoing in Kansas City. "We were both excited by the lines and the architecture, and we both wanted that kind of house but we didn't think Denver had any," she says. "We were ready to move from something that took so much time and effort, like the Victorian, into something that was more spacious and had more air around it."

Hight and Fournier have filled the home with their own art and interesting furniture, despite having two active young sons who literally race through the house. "It works wonderfully for a family because of the open space; you can see or hear the children wherever you are," Fournier comments. "I knew immediately that this was a great house."

WHAT ARE USONIAN HOUSES?

After Frank Lloyd Wright's well-known Prairie School period, he turned his attention to a populist home design he called "Usonian"—an acronym for United States of North America. Like the Prairie style, these homes had low roofs and open floor plans, and they used lots of natural materials, such as brick and wood. But as models for frugality—these were developed during the Depression—they had no basements or attics and were relatively unadorned.

The Usonian houses were built slab on grade and had radiant heating. They had open carports instead of garages. Later on in the '50s, Wright developed a modular version called Usonian Automatic, which were houses designed to be constructed by the buyer out of concrete block with reinforcing steel rods. In all, more than 100 Usonians were built, and some of the most well known are the Herbert Jacobs House in Madison, Wisconsin, and the Zimmerman House in Manchester, New Hampshire.

A Bright **Outlook**

This family can have casual meals at the kitchen bar or use the dining table at the far end of the concrete block island. Counter stools are from Design Within Reach and the new ball lights are from Stanford Electric Works in Palo Alto.

Home meant a warm and cozy Craftsman bungalow to the Pfahnl family for fifteen years before they made the leap to a midcentury ranch. Bill Pfahnl, who biked past this house daily on his way to elementary school, was happy to bring his two sons and wife, Kim, back to a neighborhood that still felt very much like home.

The down-at-the-heels 1959 house they moved into had sat unsold for six months. It had a curious bump out in the bedroom where the previous owner had gained a few square feet by annexing the patio area under the projecting eaves. And the living room had an anachronistic potbellied stove and exterior planter that chopped the floor-to-ceiling window off at the knees. These had to go, pronto.

The backyard, with its stark dirt-cement-and-crumbling-retaining-wall theme, was one of the first projects—Bill wanted to get plants growing before he tackled the interior. They planted palms, put in a screening row of bamboo along the back wall, and installed a new retaining wall and the concrete pads that today house a fire pit and dining area. "We designed the space so that nothing blocked the view from the front door through the atrium and living room and out to the back fence," Bill says.

As nice as the rest of the house is, it's the living/dining/kitchen area that delivers the one-two punch when you first visit. From a closed-off kitchen that was a "horribly nonfunctional ode to cheap '70s wood cabinets and yellow tile with wide brown grout"—Kim's words—the Pfahnls took a gutsy leap and designed an open kitchen with stainless steel appliances and a cement-block island topped with SlateScape counters. The wall that's now lined with tall cabinets has a commercial-grade stainless steel backsplash and counter with an integrated sink. The family was happy to graduate from hand-me-

downs to all new appliances, including a GE Monogram refrigerator and wine cellar, a Bosch dishwasher, and Viking wall oven, restaurant-quality cooktop, warming drawer, and microwave.

"We closed up a small window where the sink is now," Bill mentions. "We blocked it off with cardboard to see if we missed it, and because it just looked out at the neighbor's fence, we decided it wasn't really a loss."

The couple had trouble locating affordable cabinets, but during a spur-of-the-moment trip to IKEA, realized the modern-furniture chain had some good-looking choices, including the Akurum line in birch and beech that they chose. The Pfahnls let the reach of the kitchen be dictated by the cabinetry, directing the IKEA installers to start at the dining room's mahogany wall and work toward the family room. That way there was no problem with fit, and they credit the crew with doing a great job in just two days.

Using cement blocks inside "was a gutsy move," Bill says, and one that tends to elicit comments from visitors. "The kitchen does everything we need it to do, and the mahogany wall warms the area up. Our teenagers can lean on the counter without worrying about it at all, and the

Below: The window that looks out on the backyard was partially blocked by an add-on brick planter when the owners bought the house. Furnishings include a Bantam sofa and Nelson cigar floor lamp from Design Within Reach, an IKEA coffee table, a generic "potato chip" chair from Scandinavian Designs, and a reissued George Nelson Sunburst clock.

Right: New mahogany paneling and a vintage Eichler photo blown up to poster size delineate the dining area. The table and buffet are from IKEA and the Design Within Reach Kyoto chairs, this time in a natural finish, match the kitchen stools. The silk-shade pendants are from Lite Line Illuminations in Los Gatos.

stainless is starting to acquire a patina. We didn't want a kitchen that was hands-off; this looks great but it's easy to live with," he concludes.

Like another home in the San Jose, California, neighborhood (see page 10), the Pfahnls chose vinyl composite tile (VCT) to floor the entire house. Since it would work well with the radiant heating and was the closest thing to the original Eichler flooring, big-picture-guy Bill knew from the outset that that's what he wanted. Kim took longer to convince.

"I thought of slate, because that's what other people were doing, or a new skim coat of concrete, even palm or bamboo. But we already had stainless steel and cement block and mahogany and birch and slate in that space. I didn't think we could do one more cold thing on the floor," she says. "Eichlers are so much about the floors, especially this model. I didn't want people exclaiming over the floor material. I didn't want the floor to be anything more than just a floor.

"We knew this house would be much different than our last, and that we could make it something special," Kim continues. "Eichlers can be scary to some people, but they're never boring. How could you not have an emotional reaction to this home?"

This San Jose Eichler sat empty on the market waiting for homeowners with a vision.

Eichlers can be **scary to some people, but they're never boring.**
how could you not **have an emotional reaction** *to this home?*

Modest Makeovers

Don't have $20,000 for a
kitchen makeover or the
lifestyle that will accommodate
a six-month remodel, but still
need good ideas for making
your ranch something special?
This chapter is for you.

Portland **Lemonade**

The couch, coffee table, and purple Bertoia Diamond chair are from a modern store no longer in business, but Hive, highbrow, Retromodern.com, and other online retailers carry both the Diamond and Bird chairs. A formerly orange Heywood-Wakefield table is next to the couch, and a dumpster chair sits by a John Coltrane poster.

"The exterior was lemon chiffon yellow—bright and glowing," says Kristin Hammond of the 1955 ranch home she and husband Matt Demarest bought in Portland, Oregon. The dramatic roofline, open layout, and glass window walls sold the couple on their Cedar Hills house, located in a neighborhood near the Nike campus where 2005 home prices range from $200,000 to $300,000.

The couple replaced two rotted posts under the foundation, had the exterior repainted, and gutted the leaking master bath before they moved in. Under the beige medium-pile carpeting in most of the house was a nice surprise: the original cork flooring in decent condition. Less wonderful was the kitchen.

Demarest thought the cabinets were probably original, but had a poorly applied polyurethane finish and were grungy with forty years of other people's crud. "Kristin didn't like them one bit, but I thought potentially they were pretty old," he says. "Then we went out looking at a place called something like 'Cabinet Warehouse Bonanza'; we walked in and all we saw were rows of the same cabinets we had in our kitchen."

"If they weren't original, to me there was no reason to keep them," Hammond says. So they measured their kitchen and drove up to IKEA in Seattle, where they plotted out a similar layout using the Abstrakt line with a white foil finish.

"We decided the red-gloss finish option would be a little edgy for resale," Hammond says. There was also a jadeite green similar to an accent wall in the kitchen. "Again, we said, 'Resale . . .,'" she laughs.

Demarest, a film editor, had worked on construction sites and had some carpentry skills, but neither were accomplished renovators. Hammond put the cabinets together and helped with drywalling. "Boy, do the guys who do drywall professionally make spreading the compound look a lot easier than it is," she remarks. Demarest adds, "It got to the point where I'm sanding and Kristin is holding the shop vac right up to the wall. It was hilarious."

Their budget was tight, so they kept their existing refrigerator but purchased a Kitchenaid dishwasher, Maytag gas range, and Broan exhaust hood, along with Formica counters and Marmoleum flooring. The latter actually took a good-size chunk of the overall budget, which they estimate at $15,000, when removing the old flooring layers involved asbestos abatement.

A few vintage pieces—a $40 Heywood-Wakefield table that was stripped of its orange paint, a plywood chair pulled out of a dumpster, and Saarinen tulip chairs that came from Hammond's grandfather's office—are augmented with midcentury reissues.

"We looked at vintage [Bertoia] Bird chairs," Demarest says. "I trolled eBay for a year or two and I was never confident with what I'd be getting. And the ones I found in person didn't do it for me—a lot of times the covers weren't in particularly good shape. If you buy a replacement cover, you're halfway to buying a new chair. Going vintage was more of an investment than we thought we could make."

Many of their new pieces are from Hive, a Portland midcentury store, and Full Upright Position, now closed. And the couple is still hoping to inherit the Florence Knoll teak conference table the tulip chairs were once paired with.

"We plan to stay quite a long time," Hammond says. "We weren't looking for a house because we want to get into the [real estate] game. We were looking for a house to make ours."

Take **Two**

This home was built in 1964 by Joseph Eichler and designed by Claude Oakland. It has four bedrooms and two baths. The front entry leads to a private, open atrium with sliding glass doors that access a bedroom, the loggia off the living room, and the family room—or "multipurpose room" in Eichler speak.

When Mickee and Ron Ferrell bought their Joseph Eichler tract home, it had an overgrown yard with 60-foot pine trees and a rotted patio cover and deck. Inside, walls were covered with floral wallpaper, and the brown shag carpeting, sliding glass doors, and windows suffered from pet damage.

Still, it was better than most of the homes the couple toured when they were house hunting in 1989. "I remember when I walked into this one it felt familiar," says Mickee, who lived in an Eichler as a kid. "The house my parents rented always felt comfortable to me—maybe it was the open floor plan."

Ron works in construction, so he did much of the initial renovation. To accommodate their existing modern furniture and tight budget, the Ferrells went with laminate cabinets and countertops in the kitchen, and installed vinyl flooring in the kitchen and family room. Had they known what they do about Eichlers today, they probably would have had the original concrete stained and polished. They also painted the mahogany paneling. "People would take me out and flog me now, but at the time it seemed reasonable because everything was so damaged," Ron says.

At first they relished the cleanliness, but after slowly discovering the historical significance of Eichler homes, they decided they'd gone overboard and ended up with a modern house that was a tad sterile. "That really didn't fit the house any better than the [previous owner's] country style," Mickee admits.

So three years ago they changed the color scheme to more subdued neutrals, and played up the architecture by painting the beams to contrast with the tongue-and-groove ceilings. They added a pool and custom-designed awning in the back, and replaced the painted paneling with new mahogany panels in the dining room and multi-purpose room, warming up the interior. In the kitchen they upgraded to Brazilian granite countertops and mahogany book-matched cabinets, and bought a new refrigerator and dishwasher. Still, a stock aluminum slider window over the sink came from Home Depot and cost $120. Flooring in this latest renovation includes maple engineered hardwood in the kitchen and family room, Berber carpeting in the living room, and slate off the atrium entry.

Now the Ferrells feel their house and its mix of vintage and new furnishings is just right for them. "We would be happy to be here for a long time," says Mickee.

Above: Located just off the atrium and adjacent to the kitchen, the family room's flooring and mahogany paneling is new. A few pieces of rattan furniture got the Ferrells started on collecting tiki memorabilia and launched "The Rincon Room," a laundry-room-turned-tiki-bar (see page 174).

Facing: The mahogany paneling in the dining area is new but similar to what was in the house originally. The furnishings include a coffee table from Plummers and a retro-style couch, along with a vintage Majestic floor lamp, a reissued George Nelson saucer bubble lamp, and Danish modern dining table, chairs, and buffet.

A Light **Touch**

Above: The decorative display niche and clerestory-like opening in the new wall between the living and dining room improve both of the spaces.

Facing: In this Eichler in Orange, California, an IKEA rug grounds a minimalist seating arrangement that includes a wire Bertoia Diamond chair and a Danish modern torchère. Both the vintage contract seating bought on eBay and Modernica bubble lamp hanging over it were designed by George Nelson.

The Jarretts' home we saw in the three kitchen comparison on page 74 also had challenges in other parts of the 2,036-square-foot home. Sand-textured paint in several rooms, faux-oak baseboards, and industrial carpeting glued to the cement slab needed to be remedied, yet the busy family didn't have the time, money, or inclination to do a stem-to-stern remodel.

After pulling up the carpeting and evaluating the original Philippine mahogany paneling, they were faced with two dilemmas: should they go with cork, linoleum, bamboo, or terrazzo floors, or stick with the Pergo that had been installed in the hall and multipurpose room off the kitchen? And should they refinish or replace the wall paneling?

"It's tricky: What lengths do you want to go to save the original stuff?" Jon Jarrett asks somewhat rhetorically. Concluding that the painted paneling was unsalvageable, the couple chose 1/4-inch-thick Honduran mahogany, pricey at around $40 per sheet. "Lots of places stock the Luan variety, but I wasn't happy with the quality," he says. "I stood a few Honduran ones up and saw that the grain pattern was really pretty and was going to look sharp." He finished the panels with orange flake shellac cut with alcohol, then knocked back the sheen by sanding lightly with a Scotch-Brite pad.

They elected to extend the engineered floor into the living room and dining room. As for the nasty sand-texture paint, "It was one of those bad ideas from a home improvement program that shows a quick way to beautify your home," Jon surmises. "We had to pay good money to have someone scrape it off with a heat gun and a spatula."

The dining room of their Eichler model is broken up with doors to the living room, side yard, garage, and water heater. "Jon had the idea to make a clerestory wall between the living and dining rooms," Gayle Jarrett says. "I wasn't sure if we should mess with the original plan, but it made such a difference. It really adds to the room and looks original."

Rock **Solid**

A mix of styles appeals to this resident, who has a 1940s British bookcase near the front door and a large, circa-1910 table from St. Louis. The pottery was done by his mother, Pam Koush, and the upholstered chairs, ottomans, and couch are from a Houston department store.

Built in 1950 from lightweight concrete bricks similar to cinder blocks, even the roof and ceiling of architect Ben Koush's Houston home are made of cement. This is one house that isn't going anywhere in a hurricane.

"The material weighs a lot less than cinder block, and the aggregate is quite big so there's a lot of airspace; it has really good insulation value," Koush says.

He was attracted to the "Century Built" house designed by Allen Williams for its unique architecture and near-original condition. The price didn't hurt either: $112,000 in 2004. Koush bought the ranch from the daughters of the original owners, a family who lived in it for forty years before renting it out. The women were happy to find a buyer who appreciated their childhood home.

The 1,600-square-foot structure had some incongruous original touches like medieval iron straps on the front door, wrought-iron railing on the porch, and a rustic mailbox. The previous owners liked the house and the solid way it was built, but didn't feel the need for modern accessories or furnishings.

Koush's fairly modest renovation included central air, slate flooring, new paint inside and out, roofing work, and installing a new sink, counters, stove, faucets, and lighting in the kitchen. The boldest change was to open the former AstroTurf-and-wicker sunroom to the living room by putting in a beam in the opening between the two rooms.

"The structural engineer said I would need a steel beam across the top, not just wood, because the building material was so heavy," Koush says. "He suggested having pipe columns buried in the wall to hold it up, but I wanted it to all be exposed and make it clear what I've added. I specified a steel I-beam with welded flanges for that Case Study look."

The young architect changed out the home's parquet flooring in favor of an elaborate slate pattern that challenged the building crew. His CAD drawing turned out to be a "go-by" since the home's actual measurements were off a little, plus smaller honed tiles had to be sloped to align properly with the larger, thicker natural slate tile. But the international-born construction crew recognized and appreciated the home's solid building methods from concrete structures they knew from their native Mexico and Bosnia.

Although Koush isn't a slave to the period, some details are right out of the '50s. He liked and kept his metal Youngstown kitchen cabinets, cleaning them up with sprayed-on white conversion paint, and when stainless steel counters proved too expensive, he got the idea for red laminate by looking at shelter magazines of the era. While he passed on installing a dishwasher since he didn't want to tear out any of the original cabinetry, he splurged on Dornbracht faucets for the Home Depot resin sink.

Outside, the old, cracked driveway was replaced with a ribbon drive called for on the original plans. The decades-old neighborly four-foot-high chain link fence is still in place, and the contractor convinced Koush that even his tar and gravel roof was something special.

"My roofer wouldn't let me get rid of the existing slag gravel," Koush comments. After the repairs were done, the material was re-spread on the sloping roof. "He said it's from old coal-fired iron furnaces in Pennsylvania and unlike gravel you can buy today, it's flat so it doesn't blow away. You can't get materials like that anymore."

Facing: The former sunroom was opened up to the living room with an I-beam-supported doorway.

Left: This concrete block Houston midcentury was built in 1950. There are only one or two others like it in the area.

Above: The homeowner got the idea for the red laminate counters from a kitchen in a 1950 *House & Garden* magazine.

Blowing Off **the Roof**

The previous owner had added a peaked roof to this flat-roof Anshen and Allen-designed Eichler, similar to another one down the street. The current homeowners tore it off and re-created the missing beams and pergola.

"I thought, 'Barf! This is the worst looking house I've ever seen,'" says Loni Nagwani, a San Jose realtor who specializes in Eichlers and has seen plenty of butchered midcentury homes in her day. The one in question was a flat-roof 1958 Anshen and Allen design with an awkward gable roof slapped on top. This was the previous owner's attempt to put an end to leaks and add insulation, a move that other residents up and down the block took as well. Still, Loni wanted to check out the home to see if there was anything original inside that she could show some clients who were just closing on their own Eichler.

"From the minute I stepped in, it was over; I forgot to breathe. I was running through the house and saw all of the mahogany and that everything was original. I thought, 'I'll just take the roof off,'" she says.

Loni and her husband, Bharat, did just that, then upgraded the electrical system, installed skylights, and reroofed with rigid foam for the insulation value and tar and gravel for the aesthetics. Beams that had been sawed off were re-created and a missing front arbor rebuilt. They also put in black slate floors, painted the interior and exterior, renovated the mahogany paneling, and furnished with a mix of contemporary modern, midcentury reissues, and a few vintage pieces.

Loni was thrilled to have the original sliding closet doors that are often missing in Eichlers, as well as every fixture, knob, and switch plate. "It's so much easier taking off a roof than piecing all of those things together. You end up having to scrap the idea [of originality] because you just can't find a whole house of switch plate covers that match," she says.

Below: Furnishings in the family room off the kitchen include a Daphne sofa, an illuminated Toto cube lamp, a George Nelson platform bench, and a plastic version of the Eames shell chair with Eiffel Tower base, all from Design Within Reach. A "potato chip" chair, a gray coffee table from Pure Design, and a painting by Judy Gittelsohn round out the room.

Facing: The simple brick fireplace and mahogany paneling are original, and a green upholstered Danish modern armchair came with the house. New elements include the slate floors, an IKEA couch, a custom credenza that incorporates vintage Eichler frosted glass, and a Shag print over the fireplace.

Facing right: The kitchen has an artful blend of original and new elements for a unique look that's stylistically appropriate while fully functional.

With that problem in mind, Loni has become the local "Eichler parts lady," rescuing and storing an original kitchen island, Thermador cooktops and ovens, lights, hardware, and countless components thereof in her garage to pass along to other owners in need. "I'm from the Midwest, and I would cry before I'd waste something that I know one of my clients would give up their first-born for," she explains.

Eichlers were always cheaper than other houses in this upscale San Jose neighborhood, but now they are the same or more expensive. In 2005 they're commanding $800,000 to $875,000, and the homes are likely to need a fair amount of work. Gone are the days when no one wanted these ugly modern houses.

"In our Fairglen tract, neighbors may shame you into doing the right thing by your house," she says. "But you automatically have something in common with your neighbor and that starts many a conversation about resources, and that leads to a glass of wine . . ."

Pure Fun

If you're looking for houses that challenge your notion of tasteful neutral interiors and iconic furnishings, check out these examples. They may make you laugh or groan, but then again, you might just fall for some of their colorful, lighthearted fun.

Hover **Craft**

Mushroom or spaceship? Organic or futuristic? Depending on your answer, you may be channeling Disneyland's Monsanto House of the Future, John Lautner's Chemosphere House, or Alice in Wonderland's psychedelic fungus adventure. In any case, this 1964 concrete and glass home with a scalloped, wavy roof certainly epitomizes the optimism of postwar architecture.

"Either people really get it or they don't understand it at all," says owner Einar Johnson. "To me it's a groovy '60s bachelor pad—kind of Dean Martin visits *The Jetsons.* The first piece of furniture I bought for it was a bar."

Tucked into a hillside neighborhood in Laguna Niguel, California, the 1,800-square-foot "Horizon House" was designed by architect George Bissell as a demonstration house for the Portland Cement Association and the local gas company. A central core of umbrella-shaped, curved wooden beams supports the concrete roof and contains the furnace, plumbing, and electrical systems. Each of the rooms—a kitchen, living/dining space, bedroom, bath, and a den/guest room—is pie shaped, and almost the entire outside perimeter is glass. Three "infinity" walls of vertically stacked block begin outside, punch through the full-height glass and form non-weight-bearing partition walls inside. Talk about an open floor plan.

Johnson and his wife, Pat Gough, bought Horizon House as a second home in 2005; their main residence is a 1960s Ray Kappe house in the Hollywood Hills. Stanley Goodrich, the long-time previous owner, liked a more private atmosphere and had shutters on the windows to guard against sun damage to the furnishings. When he bought the house in 1992, there was carpet on the concrete floors, and closets that appear to be add-ons in both of the bedrooms. Still in place then and now is an inner circle of aggregate flooring that rings the biomorphic fireplace and continues into the original bath. Gough and Johnson aim to take the house back to as close to original as possible, recently completing phase one of that plan.

either people really **get it** *or they don't understand it at all . . .*
to me it's a **groovy '60s bachelor pad—**

kind of **Dean Martin** *visits* ***The Jetsons.***

Facing: The '60s built-in
gas stove has a pull-out
drawer for the four burners.
The white Formica counters
are original as well.

Above: The curved wall
behind the bed was refaced
with walnut-patterned
Formica, and the vertical
block was freed from its
drywall covering.

The shutters came down and carpet came up on day one, followed by grinding and polishing the concrete slab—a two-week process. In the kitchen, the couple's crew did some investigation and discovered walnut-patterned Formica under the turquoise and white paint. That helped set the tone for the renovation: "Whenever in doubt, go original," says Johnson.

Not all of the Formica survived the architectural archeology, though: partition walls in the kitchen and master bedroom had to be resurfaced, and new kitchen cabinet doors needed to be made. Gough found fifteen sheets of the discontinued walnut-color laminate warehoused in St. Louis and had them shipped out.

The home's cement block walls had been drywalled prior to Goodrich's tenure, or in the case of the kitchen, covered with thin faux bricks; the crew spent much time bringing the block back to close-to-original condition. "Once they popped off the decorative brick in the kitchen, they had to take a chisel and go down the mortar lines of the cement block and tap out the excess mortar," explains Gough. "That took two guys two weeks to do."

After a renovation of about six weeks, the couple turned to the fun of furnishing. "When we first moved into the Kappe house I was at that stage where our home was IKEA-ville," says Gough. Then about ten years ago, she went to a 1960s furniture auction in Los Angeles.

The homeowners consider the concrete floors to be an art gallery for their various area rugs. A long sectional couch bought on eBay is separated for use in the living room; the white vinyl was in good condition, so just the cushions needed re-upholstering.

"That was my first real exposure to an entire warehouse of '60s furniture. It just hit me that I had to re-create that kind of look in my home," she says. "We pretty much knew that's what we'd want to do in the Laguna house, too, but make it more of a swinging bachelor pad with the low couch and sparse furniture. The look was driven by the concrete floors and glass walls; it was a no-brainer for me." Phase two will involve restoration of the windows now blocked by the bedroom closets and rebuilding the freestanding closets shown in the original plans—this time in walnut instead of the specified teak and Formica. A second bath added by Goodrich off the kitchen near the carport will stay.

"A round house is so unique," Johnson says. "We're all raised to live in boxes and it's taken me a couple of months to get the intuitive feel of a round house. When I first put furniture in, everything was focused inward toward the fireplace; that's what you're trained to do in a box house. After a while I realized the whole flow is from the in to the out; I rearranged the furniture to be much more outward looking now."

"I miss it terribly—the serenity and energy of the house," says former owner Goodrich longingly. "The reason why I bought my condo in Palm Springs is because it had one curved wall and reminded me of the Horizon House."

Belarus on the **Bayou**

Above: The unassuming
exterior of this Houston
ranch house does little to
prepare guests for the wild
and crazy interior.

Facing: The team that
designed this remodel say
they try to avoid any par-
allel or perpendicular
lines, and work triangular
shapes into their projects
whenever possible.

One Christmas Rita and Yuri Katchan and their seven-year-old daughter came from Minsk to Houston to visit friends. They had just one carry-on bag stuffed with a few belongings and the towels they'd been advised to bring, since this was reputedly an item in short supply in the United States. That was 1992 and they've been here ever since.

Yuri, a mechanical engineer, took an unassuming midcentury brick ranch house, and in three months turned it into something unlike any other. Working with Victor Kagan, the friend the Katchans came to visit and a partner in a remodeling company the two men formed, the pair deconstructed the house to its essence and then layered wild finishes on surprising angles—and then some.

The three-bedroom, two-bath home was vacant and had been a rental in recent years. "The first time I saw the house, I made an offer to the seller in about an hour," Yuri says. "It was what I was looking for. The location was good and I love houses with a flat roof and a lot of open space. It wasn't structurally too complicated. It had a nice big backyard.

"I never had my own house or apartment in Russia," he continues. "We always lived with our parents. [Their home] was no particular style; it was just a small place to spend the night."

A partition wall between the narrow sliver of a dining area and the living room was replaced with load-bearing columns painted four different colors. The big-box kitchen— "plain, cheap, basic, boring" in Victor's estimation—was gutted. Their new kitchen has

IKEA cabinets but looks custom with its angled walls, tile mosaics, triangular soffits, inlaid countertops, and a handmade door with decorative blue glass portholes—votive candle holders inset into the wood as it turns out. The master bathroom gained a glass-block shower that bumps out of the home's footprint, along with a whirlpool tub and Yuri's signature textured plasterwork and intricate tile installations.

"A lot of our friends believe that we are not completely normal," says Victor, an electrical engineer, with dry amusement. "Not crazy, but at least strange. A neighbor came over and wanted to know how we came up with all of these ideas. Had we been smoking something? We told him, no, we don't do that; we're Russian so we *will* have a couple of Jacks on the rocks—that helps to get good ideas."

Both men enjoy the challenges of framing out unusual walls, and Yuri is the patient one who meticulously made the intersections of hardwood and tile meet seamlessly. Typically Victor

sketches out an idea, and then Yuri works up CAD drawings so the engineering pair know exactly how they'll approach a specific project.

"We use materials and techniques that initially might have totally different applications," says Victor. "We like to play with granite and marble and ceramics and glass and metal inserts on walls and floors."

Rita, a computer software specialist, was out of the country for some of the remodel. She left the decisions to Victor and Yuri. "I really trust Yuri and his taste. He can't live in a space that's not friendly and he can never stop working on this house. But I do kind of hate it when they come up with a new idea because I know they're going to drop right now whatever they're doing and start something new. They're really good together; very creative."

"I don't like boring, plain walls," Yuri confirms somewhat unnecessarily. "I always like to bring unusual shapes to a house. I did just what I see in my mind; it makes me happy when I'm home."

Left: The kitchen hardly looks like an **IKEA** special with its custom finishes and layered details.

Above: The new master bath has a glass-block shower area that pops out of the original footprint. The decorative tile installation was done using remnants.

Juice **It Up**

This couple was thinking of the dentist offices of their childhood when they found this bamboo mural wallpaper and decided to slather it throughout their guest bedroom. The burlap ceiling treatment is intended to give the impression of sleeping in a tent.

Thanks to their cult following, even the most bastardized post-and-beam Eichler can elicit a bidding war. Four years ago Steve and Jenn Lewis were lucky to find a 1962 model that needed work, but whose potential was still apparent under years of neglect.

The original owners had taken good care of the house, but subsequent residents drained the pool—which caused the plaster to crack and cost $7,000 to repair—and constructed a solid wall around the front door where Eichlers typically have opaque glass. Right on schedule after the home's one-year warranty expired, the rainy season arrived and with it roof problems. "Water was coming in through the ceiling slats and the vents; the roof was just pocketed with holes," Steve says.

His one regret surrounding the purchase was going with a home inspector out of the Yellow Pages. "By tens of thousands of dollars, it was the biggest mistake I made," he says. "Everything about this house was bad: the air conditioner compressor was out, there had been a heating leak in the slab with a repair that routed the pipe on top of the floor at the base of the kitchen counter. Another leak shorted out an electrical outlet in the living room floor, which later caused a fire that Jenn caught just in time."

After fixing myriad problems, the young couple began to fill the house with their own take on "deviant decor." "I like things that are obnoxious but not offensive," Steve says. "Kind of *Boogie Nights* meets Laughlin, Nevada."

Examples of their style include a beauty parlor hairdryer chair sitting on the AstroTurf surrounding their pool, a smoky acrylic dining set, lava lamps, an eight-track/radio/record player that strobes in time with the beat, a lounge-lizard couch in the family room, and "rain" lamps that drip oil down monofilament for that classy waterfall effect. Favorite sources are

Left: This Eichler multipurpose room off the kitchen is ready for a retro party anytime with its tasty decor.

Below: Who wouldn't want to sip a cocktail from a beauty shop chair on poolside AstroTurf?

Facing: The swinging plastic dining set was found at a vintage shop in Arizona, while the teak storage unit holding collectibles such as barware and lava lamps is a family heirloom.

Las Vegas and Palm Springs thrift stores, where entire households of vintage items appear; Out of Vogue in Fullerton, California, which Jenn says has "amazing '60s and '70s stuff"; and Go-Kat-Go in Phoenix, Arizona, where the couple found the dining table and chairs, a hula-girl bead curtain dividing the kitchen and dining room, and a sputnik lamp for their grasshopper-green hall.

Then there's the guest bedroom papered in a bamboo mural from floor to ceiling, including the closet and hallway doors. "In a normal house, the bamboo room would be kind of ridiculous," Steve admits. "Here it doesn't seem as crazy. There's a weird creative freedom built into the house that allows things like AstroTurf around the pool. It looks ridiculous to have a disco ball in the atrium, but it would look far more ridiculous in almost any other house."

Rock 'em **Sock 'em Color**

Above: Although the facade is typical of a zillion others, the interior of this ranch house is anything but in its use of color.

Facing: The traditional living room has been transformed with vibrant color and an exuberant mix of flea-market finds and vintage-inspired new furniture.

The owners of more traditional ranches are every bit as proud as their counterparts in Modernist homes. But sometimes the more staid details—hardwood floors, crown molding, wall-to-wall carpeting, double-hung windows, classical fireplace mantels—seem to call out for formal furnishings that don't do a thing for young buyers drawn to midcentury design. How about an industrial-strength shot of color?

Dan and Jennifer Harrison faced just this challenge in their 1954 ranch built on a street nicknamed "Doctors' Row" in Anaheim, California. They knew bungalows, having lived in a 1920s cottage replete with colorful collectibles for several years, but when they doubled their square footage, they were at a bit of a loss on how to furnish and decorate their 2,600-square-foot ranch.

None of the paint shades they'd had in their bungalow seemed to look good in the new house. "I liked those colors so much that I thought I'd just bring them here," Jennifer says. "Nothing that was tried and true worked."

Custom built on a lot and a half, the house has only two bedrooms, but they're enormous. The living room and kitchen are similarly spacious, while the dining room and den are more typical sizes. Two baths in virtually original condition, plenty of storage, a pool, and a bonus room in the garage sealed the deal for the couple.

"When we lived in the bungalow I was proud to have a home from the '20s. Anything later than that was too new," Jennifer says. "But when we walked into this house, the charm and the thought that went into it [struck me]. It's like this is the evolution of homes: a bungalow is plunked in the middle of a yard, while this home wraps around the yard. There was not one place I could sit in our bungalow and look out and enjoy the yard. Here, every window has a great view. It's so well planned."

Visitors immediately comment on the paint and furniture colors. Jennifer is the force behind the color scheme, and while Dan admits he wouldn't necessarily have picked these hues, he's fully onboard. "We wanted the den to be a vibrant color, yet soothing. We went back and forth between cool colors and warm colors; we finally found this awesome coral," he says.

The living room was more of a challenge. "We went through some disastrous shades," Dan remembers. "Everything was way too light; it looked like a fishbowl. We tried seafoam green, peach, and light blue. A friend suggested this purple color but we thought it was way too dark. Then we started thinking that the room is really well lit during the day, plus it's huge. If you paint a small room dark it's going to feel like the walls are caving in, but in a big room, why not—give it a shot."

Left: Color and detail, from the sputnik light fixture to the wall colors and Heywood-Wakefield dining set, grab your eye. You don't even notice that the wall-to-wall carpeting is beige.

Below: The homeowners labored over finding just the right colors for each room and making sure that they all worked together, albeit in a super-vibrant fashion.

Bottom: The owners love their bathroom's period tile and just painted and accessorized to complement it.

Their furniture and collections run from 1930s Fiestaware and a 1954 Heywood-Wakefield dining set to current Todd Oldham chairs. "In a lot of homes you can tell the owners picked out pieces specifically for a given place—I need an Eames chair or Noguchi table right there," Dan says. "Everything is pure. That's not how we are. We like the '30s and the '40s and the '50s and the '60s, and things that are brand new. We want to keep things in a retro style, but be comfortable, too. We want it to feel like a home, not a museum."

While their bungalow lent itself to displays everywhere, in this house more things are stored behind closed doors, like Jennifer's Pyrex, toaster, and pottery collections. "People said the other house was Pee-Wee's Playhouse; this house is like 'Toontown grows up,'" Jennifer says. "It feels like such an adult house."

Gallery **Opening**

Peter Blank confesses he's always been a loft guy, and one look around his A-frame modern ranch in Denver confirms he must have spent a lot of time in art galleries as well. "From the street it was unassuming, so when I walked in the door and looked at the living room, I saw that the bones of this house were so great," he says. "I knew this would be such a cool space if you were to take it to the next level. It spoke to me; your spirit just soars when you walk in."

The 1956 home was part of an H. B. Wolff development, a company that local rumor has it was sued by Joseph Eichler for knocking off his designs. The tract of about 100 Modernist houses was planned to be larger than its three-block radius, Blank says, but instead, traditional small ranches surround the area.

A previous owner altered the 1,630-square-foot residence; what is now a flat-roof enclosed entry with an office behind it was originally a carport, and the garage to the left is an add-on as well. But the striking part is the A-frame roof, one of only five such homes in the tract. When Blank bought the house, the seller was finishing up a renovation that added traditional elements such as paneled doors, brass hardware, and other touches he finds to be "Cape Cod-ish." Some of these are on Blank's punch list to undo in upcoming years.

His desire to take the house to the next level included extending the living room and kitchen footprints to enclose a small patio, which gave the massive wood posts and cement footings that make up the A-frame structure a starring role in the interior architecture. He also put in a new kitchen that includes a partition wall of rich cherry paneling that he terms a "mosaic with wood."

Facing: The kitchen's green breakfast nook area was added when a patio was enclosed, resulting in more square footage both here and in the living room, visible through the countertop pass-through.

Above right: This Denver midcentury combines an A-frame core with a flat-roof section that was originally a carport. The garage is a later addition.

"The paneling has a '60s retro feel to it. I wanted the depth of cherrywood but enough red and brown to play off the floors; the staining process took about a month," Blank says. "The corners were particularly challenging: two pieces just meeting up wasn't a very clean look, so I ended up creating a corner piece to finish it off."

In the kitchen itself, he chose a black-and-white linoleum floor, counters of butcher block, stainless steel, and Silestone—a European surfacing material made of quartz and epoxy that is harder than granite—and gallery-worthy lighting. The white walls he originally specified felt too stark, so Blank and his painter developed a green mellowed with eight different glaze applications. The cabinets and hardware are from Home Depot, the microwave from Target, and other appliances include a GE Profile refrigerator and a Thermador stove and hood.

"People might argue that some of what I've done isn't good for resale, but I chose to do this for my own personal enjoyment," says Blank, a Denver realtor. "The next person will probably paint the kitchen walls white again, but while I'm here I want to enjoy it."

In the last year Blank has sold three houses in the neighborhood and he feels that people really buy architecture, not a furniture showroom. "I don't believe furnishings should compete with the architecture. Big heavy furniture in a small house of 1,000 square feet is not going to work," he says, "but if you do platform beds, low seating and '50s and '60s-style furniture, those work exceptionally well. That furniture was made for this type of environment. You have to be more of a minimalist."

Blank knows from experience the pain of rethinking your style and divesting yourself of "stuff," having downsized from his massive loft furnishings—big armoires, large sectionals, and expansive cocktail tables. His previous residence had twice the square footage of this home, and he says he brought only artwork and a bed with him when he moved.

The artwork includes paintings and ceramics from Colorado artists, as well as rugged sugarcane grinders from the Philippines that work as sculpture in the living room, black clay pots from Vietnam, and geodes and amethyst crystals from Brazil. "People give me grief about the cowhide in the main room, but I grew up in Brazil and they were very commonplace on hardwood floors," Blank says. "The furnishings in the living room are a culmination of where I grew up and where I've been."

The single homeowner says his distinctive space is perfect for cocktail parties, and that he purposely didn't install a dining table inside, preferring to host gatherings where guests mingle to enjoy finger food and cocktails. "I really believe in having good architecture and good lighting and good music," he says. "It creates a sexy space."

Imagining the **Past**

Above: Carter Sparks, an architect at Anshen and Allen, designed most of the Streng Bros. homes built in California.

Facing: Repeating neutrals, such as the shades of taupe seen in the Natuzzi chairs, rug, fireplace, and decorative masks, pulls disparate elements together in this family room.

If this house puts you in mind of Disneyland, with its colorful interior and Enchanted Tiki Room backyard, there's a good reason for that: Paul Torrigino and Richard Gutierrez were theme-park ride designers for Disney before decamping for Sacramento, California.

The 1962 house they found was part of a tract of Streng Bros. Homes, Eichler look-alikes built in Sacramento and Davis, California, in the late '50s and early '60s. Architect Carter Sparks, who worked at the Eichler-affiliated architectural firm of Anshen and Allen for several years, designed most of the company's 3,000-plus Modernist homes.

Jim and Bill Streng eschewed Eichler's open-roof atriums and radiant heating in their models, but air-conditioning was part of the package in this climate of hot summers. Strengs run between 1,800 and 2,200 square feet, and share aggregate paving and spherical light fixtures with their Eichler first cousins.

The Gutierrez/Torrigino house was carpeted throughout, had cottage cheese ceilings, and countrified decor. On the plus side, previous owners had pushed out the back of the family room in an architecturally appropriate manner, and with the sellers living elsewhere part of the year, the house had been lightly used.

"When we moved here we weren't looking for a modern house," Torrigino comments. "We were just looking for an affordable house. We happened to see this one and we fell in love with the kitchen, so we just jumped in."

That nostalgic kitchen still has its original GE appliances that the couple says work like a dream. "When we first saw this low counter [between the kitchen and family room] we thought we would build it up. But we do breakfast buffets and martini parties; it's perfect for that," Torrigino says. "I'm glad we didn't alter it right away."

"I saw a picture of Bill Streng at his house in Davis, and he has the same counter in his own kitchen," Gutierrez adds.

Below: Appliances, countertops, and cabinetry are all original in this 1962 Sacramento, California, home. The previous owners pushed the dining area and adjoining family room out several feet, but the addition looks seamless.

Facing: Retro meets contemporary: a '70s buffet holds barware, tiki accessories, and caricature sculptures made by the homeowners. Copenhagen Furniture in Sacramento was the source for the Italian table and chairs, while the '60s red lamp was bought on eBay.

The pair sanded the dark brown cabinet bodies and refinished with a cherry stain, then painted the doors green and orange, but "it looked like a pack of Wrigley's spearmint gum," Torrigino admits. The addition of a few white doors worked to soften it. "Most people have remodeled their kitchens in this neighborhood, and they all have waist-high tile or granite counters, but there is nothing wrong with this," he says.

The partners had ceramic tile installed on the floors and began to furnish the three-bedroom home. "We had not one stick of modern furniture when we moved here," Torrigino says. "We debated whether to use actual period furniture and make it look like it was really 1962, or to get new stuff, which is nicer, you don't have to restore it, and it's more in scale. We found we really liked new stuff."

A sofa and chairs from Natuzzi and reissued pieces from midcentury designers such as Eileen Gray, George Nelson, and Isamu Noguchi are in the family room. The guest room/office has a Crate & Barrel bed that looks decidedly tropical in the yellow, peach, and blue-schemed space decorated with caricature sculptures made by Torrigino.

"That's the nice thing about modern furniture now; so much of it has that '60s style to it," Gutierrez says. Their home combines contemporary, kitsch—"I Love Lucy" dishes in a framed shadow box and "The Dating Game"-esque daisies on their TV room wall—and baroque antiques, but they can see other ways that the house could have gone.

"Sixties kitsch furniture would work in this house, as would low-slung rattan for a tropical Polynesian theme," Torrigino says. "The big beams are very much like a tiki hut; I can see bamboo woven wall coverings."

"This style of house is really a blank canvas," Gutierrez adds. "I don't particularly like the ultramodern stark look, but it really works in these homes, too. The architecture doesn't fight with what you do."

Outside the **Ranch**

A midcentury ranch house often comes to a new owner with exterior baggage: overgrown junipers and rampaging ivy obliterate the lines of the house, and aging lawns struggle under the shade of mature trees. Maybe it was the recipient of an '80s English cottage garden or simply had "zeroscape" thanks to a seller with a brown thumb. See how these homeowners coped with their challenges.

The Midcentury Landscape

Accessible from two bed-
rooms, a private garden at
a Cliff May home has a
small fountain and plant-
ings of New Zealand flax
and society garlic.

Vintage house plan books typically showed traditional plantings in their illustrations: a swath of lawn with a sapling specimen tree, foundation plantings, and maybe a cheerful window box or bright annuals bordering the front walkway. When owners moved into their brand-new homes, more often than not they faced an expanse of bare earth and the same question you face now: "What should I do with my yard?"

The two names most commonly associated with the California school of modern garden design are Garrett Eckbo and Thomas Church. Eckbo was inspired by abstract art and brought architecture into the garden through curving walls, fences, hardscape, and pergolas. He treated plants as sculpture and designed the public portions of Gregory Ain's Culver City, California, Mar Vista Housing development in the late '40s.

Similarly, landscape architect Church met designer Alvar Aalto on a trip to Europe in the late '30s, and fell for his Modernist approach. Church's asymmetrical designs, including the Greenmeadow Eichler tract in Palo Alto, featured curvilinear elements and emphasized the free flow between the home and garden. With architects such as Rudolph Schindler, Richard Neutra, John Lautner, A. Quincy Jones, and many others designing homes and tracts that embraced their sites instead of just providing a refuge from the environment, the look of Modernist gardens emerged to change the landscape of suburbia.

So the choices you face are taking your garden back to period correct, building on what you inherited from past owners, or freely interpreting a hybrid of the two. The exteriors of these midcentury homes show approaches that might be right for you, but we encourage you to use them as a springboard and tailor plantings to suit your climate and gardening abilities.

Landscape Hallmarks

Above: The strip of yard between the driveway and the neighboring house becomes a graphic element with its round globes and gravel in this San Jose home.

Facing: This backyard has both sunny and shady areas for Houston's variable weather.

POCKET GARDENS

Many ranch houses have three or more distinct outdoor areas that lend themselves to different treatments. A typical street facade consists of a postage-stamp-size lawn or built-in planter boxes next to the driveway and garage. Then, behind a fence or cement-block wall is the private side or backyard with a patio and access to the house through sliding glass or french doors. If there's a pool, that takes up much of the room in this space. Last are the narrow walkways between neighboring homes that often turn into storage areas for toys and tools, or house air-conditioning units.

Instead of presenting a problem, these discrete spaces can offer options to homeowners and lend themselves to activity-specific landscaping. The low-maintenance strip next to the driveway looks great with just raked gravel and graphic cement globes. The patio with the teak dining set and the chaise longues around the pool can have a different ambience than the pocket garden off the master bedroom—the one with a simple fountain and a comfortable chair for reading the Sunday paper. And narrow side yards can become window-framed green views with careful planning and plants suited to the site.

In a Texas home, also seen on page 24, rectangular pavers lead from an ipewood deck off the master bedroom to a cement patio with teak and metal furniture. Mondo grass is planted between the stepping-stones, and ferns, Australian violet, and creeping Jenny surround a lichen-covered stone in a planting area off the family room. Pine, magnolia, liquid amber, and yaupon trees are kept laced so that understory plants get enough light to thrive. The Japanese-esque plantings are a far cry from the grass, pine trees, sandbox, and tire swing the homeowners inherited.

Below: The square stepping stones and rectangular patio echo the lines of the modernist ranch house, while the round table and mounding plants soften the effect.

Facing left: Cement patios and retaining walls were the first priority in this San Jose garden. The opposite corner has a gas fire pit and additional seating on the retaining wall.

Facing right: Highly graphic plantings give a clean, modern look to this under-eaves area.

This San Jose Eichler has a series of small gardens: the stone, gravel, and aloe planting right next to the living room window allows the eye to travel from the entry atrium through the living room and out to the back fence without stopping. It also reminds the owners of Palm Springs' desert landscape. In another corner of the same modest-size backyard, raised rectilinear planters organize the space, contain the distinct plant groupings—including tall bamboo that offers privacy and masks an unsightly telephone pole—and repeat the cement block material used in the kitchen (see page 83).

Pools

Kidney-shaped pools were the standard bearer for years, but rectangular and lap pools look great in midcentury settings, too. Whether you're blessed with a sprawling spread like this Swiss Miss in Palm Springs, or your pool *is* essentially your backyard, it's easy to dress the space with vintage or new furniture and some bold pots of color.

Paving

Graphic contrast works particularly well in a midcentury setting. From square cement pavers set in a bed of shiny Mexican pebbles or surrounded by Scotch moss and tumbled glass, to scored cement softened by curved beds mulched with colorful gravel, the matte versus shiny and hard versus soft elements complement plantings. Though not available fifty years ago, diamond-patterned pavers and aggregate paving are handsome choices for driveways, paths, and patios.

Facing: An Alexander home with a large lot has room for a pool, covered and open patios, and a sizable lawn.

Above: The rounded planting bed mirrors the curved cement path next to this Palm Springs kidney-shaped pool.

Left: Mexican pebbles between cement stepping-stones are a classic approach.

Left below: Pavers with planting pockets make for a driveway or path that absorbs rainfall and cuts down on runoff.

Facing: The dining patio offers all the comforts of home, and more room than the interior kitchen table, in this atypical Eichler model.

Below: This midcentury furniture collector uses his side patio as another display and living area.

Below right: The Japanese elements work well in this Mediterranean climate garden.

Rooms With a View

Midcentury ranches are particularly adept at blurring the line between indoors and out. The patio of this ranch mirrors the carport architecture on the opposite side and has sunny and shaded portions for Denver's unpredictable weather. Vintage midcentury furniture and a graphic privacy fence expand the living space, a necessity for the less than 1,000-square-foot home. In San Jose, a fully covered ceramic tile patio offers another dining and entertainment space for an Eichler with a small table and chairs inside.

The view from the patio at this Cliff May home is of an Asian-inspired front garden that's screened from the street by a six-foot fence. Raked gravel, statues of Buddha, and a one-person teahouse were fit in around the existing palm trees and hibiscus.

Minimizing **Hardscape**

Above: This modest ranch has been updated with french doors and the backyard freed of its excessive hardscape.

Facing: The new planting pocket softens the view from the back patio off the kitchen. The garage architecture is consistent with its bungalow neighborhood.

In Monrovia, California, architect Mark Houston's 1955 ranch was infill housing when it was built in a 1920s neighborhood. His traditional home is L-shaped, and previously the backyard was a sea of concrete. Recently he enclosed a carport and turned it and half of his two-car garage into living space, gaining another 800 square feet for his family. The real trick for the remodel was to give the long, narrow yard room for plantings while accommodating a driveway to the garage areas.

"The concept was to replace the reflective, hot concrete and soften the yard so that when you look out from the dining room and kitchen you almost don't see any hardscape," Houston says.

The city dictated that he build an additional one-car garage, which he designed to look like a stand-alone barn. "I didn't want to continue with the stucco of the house when I added the garage," he says. "The planning department wanted me to bring the same roofline straight back; I had to refuse—that leg of the L would have been too long."

Immediately adjacent to the kitchen is a resurfaced concrete patio with a teak dining table and chairs and a clay chiminea to ward off the evening chill. Two steps down is a small pocket garden that was once part of the concrete drive, but now has a flagstone path, boulders, and plantings that include a young sycamore tree, New Zealand flax, roses, yarrow, English thyme groundcover, and a bower vine espaliered along the wall of the family room. At the very back of the property is a modest expanse of lawn.

"The perspective is such that you now see the patio and the greenery and not the driveway beyond," Houston says. "And from the family room's french doors, you get a view of shrubs and the sycamore tree—it's a nice, refreshing feeling. It's the hub and does wonders for the backyard."

Midcentury Looks: **Different Climates**

Above: This Denver home's streetscape is very appealing with its sculptural junipers and pockets of perennials.

Facing left: A recirculating manmade stream contained by rusting I-beams burbles across the existing patio.

Facing right: The challenges of a steep site called for plantings that didn't need to be mowed and were low-maintenance. Succulents and grasses add color and texture, while tough prostrate rosemary makes for a bulletproof groundcover.

As stylistically fitting as palm trees, succulents, and gravel are, that approach isn't right for many homes and climates. In Denver, two neighbors have markedly different looks. The front yard of the ranch house above came with majorly overgrown junipers and a pine tree shading the front facade. Becky Miller trimmed the tree and shrubs so their sculptural qualities are emphasized and installed a dry riverbed of gravel and stepping stones that separates the small lawn and perennials from the house. Color varies with the time of year, but in early summer, dark pink Jupiter's beard (Centranthus ruber), bright yellow basket-of-gold (Aurinia saxatilis), and purple Hungarian speedwell (Veronica austriaca) carry the show.

Across the street, neophyte gardener Peter Blank has built on what he inherited: the sizable lawn in back has hillocks and swales to give it interest and more of a meadow look, and a large Russian olive tree has been joined by a grove of aspen saplings underplanted with groundcover. He kept an existing brick pad and removed a portion of the cement patio to make room for a water feature edged in rusting steel. The pergola is Blank's design as well, and its angled supports mirror the post-and-beam structure of his 1956 A-frame ranch (see page 128).

At a Southern California L-shaped ranch with a prominent steep driveway, the homeowner was looking for architectural texture and interesting plants but not a lot of flower color. Landscape designer Paula Hanson was asked to retain small areas of lawn until the family's children are older, yet keep the entire property low maintenance. Both front and backyards use a limited range of plant materials, including rosemary, echeveria, kangaroo paws, Festuca ovina glauca, asparagus fern, eucalyptus 'Baby,' papyrus, Euphorbia martini, and blue oat grass.

Adding Personality

Concerned your house has that cookie-cutter tract mentality? Collections can add an extra element of interest to ranch interiors or set a theme from which the rest of the decor emerges.

Vintage and reproduction midcentury designs are a popular way to furnish and decorate, and there are lots of categories to focus on: teak Dansk ware, vintage textiles, kitschy tiki collectibles, '50s barware, Memphis-era plastics, wild lamps, '60s electronics, and lunch boxes—the possibilities are only limited by your taste, imagination, and budget. And since popular design underwent dramatic stylistic changes from the late '40s through the optimist atomic age and into the youth-oriented '70s, your home can definitely stand out from the house next door.

Mini **Marvel**

The sofa is an Edward Wormley for Dunbar; the red chair is an Eero Saarinen Womb chair, and the coffee table a reissued Isamu Noguchi design. Saarinen also designed the two Knoll pedestal tables; the walnut-top version displays pieces from Atwater Pottery on it.

Think your house is small? Try Nick Horvath and Kim Bennett's 912-square-foot "Likeler" on for size. Built in 1952 in the Harvey Park neighborhood of Denver, the midcentury modern furniture dealer and his fiancée have squeezed a ton of style into their $190,000 home.

A self-taught student of modern design, Horvath's aesthetic has evolved from his bachelor pad steel-frame-furniture days to something perhaps best described as esoteric eclectic midcentury. An Eames LTR (Low Table Rod) came out of the factory with a George Nelson label on it, a factory faux pas that makes it just a bit rarer. His Nelson bubble lamps are all vintage. And around his George Nakashima dining table—one of the studio woodworker's few commercial designs and one that was only produced for a few years—are Eero Saarinen 71 Series chairs, but not the more common upholstered versions. No, Horvath's have fiberglass backs and plywood legs, a rare and ultimately unpopular design that didn't hold up in the commercial settings they were designed for.

"I'm a label whore," he admits cheerfully. "I like to know the history and design concept behind a piece. I would much rather go to the ultimate source—an Eames chair rather than the generic chair made for the mass market."

The Noguchi coffee table and Eames Storage Unit in the compact living room are reissues, but everything else is vintage save for some accessories—ceramics from Adam Silverman at Atwater Pottery, who Horvath thinks is the next Natzler; pieces by that other pottery guy, Jonathan Adler; and some Nambe candlesticks. "I can loosen up on accessories," he says proudly.

When the couple merged households, they bought a contemporary couch and dining table, but those new items have since been passed along. Bennett came from a Crate & Barrel aesthetic and finds reissues and midcentury interpretations just fine. "I think it's cool that they're reissuing things that someone in their twenties who's up and coming could buy, something cheaper that has the look. I don't mind it," she says.

"It's a double-edged sword," Horvath adds. "It's great to see that there's such an interest and demand for this that the manufacturers are starting to answer the call, but on the other hand, everybody wants everything right now. I think some people want more the look than the history. I like pieces to have a soul, a little history, maybe a scratch or a dent."

A trip to Boomerang for Modern in San Diego, where she saw the price tags on some of the same items they had at home, convinced Bennett of the fiscal wisdom of Horvath's collection. "When I started selling my apartment furniture—which I'd spent a fortune on—I was getting a quarter of what I'd bought it for a year prior. But when Nick buys things, he makes a profit when he sells. I think I can get into this!"

With the modern reproductions available now, Horvath says the market has been brought into check a little. "Before, people were willing to pay $800 to $1,200 for a Nelson clock; now an average vintage ball or spike clock might be $400 to $500 on eBay."

His collection is focused on classic modern—Charles and Ray Eames, George Nelson, Eero Saarinen, Paul McCobb, Isamu Noguchi, Edward Wormley, studio ceramics, and Blenko art glass. "Most mid-twentieth-century-modern collectors will have their staples: everybody should have an Eames chair, a Blenko bottle, a Lightolier lamp. The rest of it is up to the collector and their own personal taste," Horvath says.

"I've been through three or four different focuses in the past few years. In a coffeehouse I had downtown, the space really lent itself to '60s mod plastic space-age design. In this house there was a period where I had a lot of Danish modern—Hans Wegner, Finn Juhl, Stig Lindberg. Any true collector is never one thing all the time. It's hard because there's so much great stuff out there."

In answer to what's next on the collecting horizon, Horvath has a couple of thoughts: "Designers tend to dictate collecting trends," he says. "Right now people are interested in Hollywood Regency—very decorative, chic, lots of mirrors. I think plastics are really going to take off, and '80s Memphis has always been hot because it's such a weird little hiccup in design history. It was this rebuttal against what was expected of modern—a goofy, whimsical, tongue-in-cheek interpretation."

As for classics such as his, "Everybody's kind of been there, done that, so they're passing on to the next trend. That's fine with me; I've always loved it and always will. If you look at auction prices, things that were going for thousands of dollars are getting a pass; that's pretty amazing. Now is the time to start buying pieces that are less popular."

The single most important thing to do is educate yourself Horvath says, advising that new collectors "buy every period design book and magazine and study them. An educated collector is a good collector. The classic pieces will always be collectible—they just fall in and out of favor. An Eames chair is a staple like a little black dress."

A small dining room next to the kitchen is chockfull of important collectibles, including a George Nakashima table and Eero Saarinen 71 Series chairs. In contrast, the flooring and other kitchen elements were created from surplus building materials.

Pull Up a **Chair**

Six of collector Peter Maunu's favorites, clockwise from the Marcel Breuer chaise longue: a vintage Mies van der Rohe Barcelona chair, reissued Neutra Boomerang chair, Jean Prouvé wood-and-metal chair, wire Bertoia Bird chair, and in the center of it all, Charlotte Perriand's milkmaid-esque stool.

Fifty-one chairs seem like a lot, but Peter Maunu still can't resist a stray by the side of the road or a good deal at a yard sale. "I realized that the architects I liked also made great furniture and, unless you're Donald Trump, you can't buy all of the architecture you admire," he says. His 1949 Modernist ranch sits on an acre of land in the foothills of Altadena, California, where he puts just about every chair to use indoors or out, particularly when he and his wife, Irmi, host a party.

A Bertoia Bird chair designed in 1952 was found in San Francisco in the early '80s for $100, which seemed like a lot at the time. Maunu loves its sculptural qualities and prefers this unpadded version. The 1942 Boomerang chair by Richard Neutra is a reissue from House Industries and was signed by Neutra's son, Dion. A bungee-cord chair the Maunus own was designed in the '20s by Rene Herbst but manufactured in the '80s, about the time the designer died.

Four other top picks from his chair parade include a Jean Prouvé task chair with green metal legs, a well-loved Barcelona chair that needs new $3,000 cushions, a European country vernacular three-legged stool designed by Charlotte Perriand, and a wood frame upholstered chaise from Marcel Breuer designed in the late '30s, according to Maunu.

The iconic Barcelona chair was part of Ludwig Mies van der Rohe's decidedly modern German Pavilion at the 1929 Barcelona International Exhibition, and the chair came to be a fixture in modern reception rooms everywhere. "I love it but there are contradictory things about it: it's too heavy, it's too expensive to make, and there's something a little elitist about it," Maunu says. "But as a form, it's one of the most elegant, beautiful chairs."

What appear to be run-of-the-mill wooden directors chairs are early models from the Telescope Casual Furniture Company, and the ubiquitous boxy white wire-mesh stacking chairs sold by every supermarket and hardware store before white resin chairs took over the galaxy don't look like anything special. But Maunu explains they're the granddaddy of the chairs you or I had—EMU Italian models—and in his mind something destined to have cachet in another decade or two.

"Right now they're too fresh in our minds. We saw them everywhere," he says. "But I think they will become classics."

Art for **Art's Sake**

In the living room, vintage '50s furniture complements the fine art. Over the fireplace is a lithograph, *Up Against It*, by Robert Arneson, and a wood and ceramic sculpture by Arthur Gonzalez hangs over the couch. Next to the club chair, a table made of LPs holds what looks like a bowl of green kids' toys—*Mixed Green Salad* by David Gilhooly.

Making, collecting, and displaying art is what Tony and Donna Natsoulas are all about. Tony, a ceramic sculptor, and his wife, Donna, looked for years to find the perfect place to showcase their collection and vintage furnishings; now they live in a 1962 Streng Bros. ranch in Sacramento with an amazing assortment of art everywhere you turn.

The collection includes works from Robert Arneson, Roy De Forest, Wayne Thiebaud, Arthur Gonzalez, Howard Finster, Fred Babb, Suzanne Adan, Jeff Koons, Andy Warhol, Tom Rippon, Heidi Bekebrede, and Clayton Bailey. Everything they display is funny, colorful, and somewhat representational—Tony's capsule assessment of their collection criteria. Walls, floors, and any horizontal surface hold something—or more likely, several somethings—to make you smile.

"We don't think of viewing art as sitting down in the living room to look at a painting," Tony says. "I'm brushing my teeth and I'm looking at something; we like to be constantly stimulated. Luckily we've picked pieces that you can keep looking at that don't turn invisible after a while."

"I look at a shelf and I think I'd like it better if it had three pieces on it instead of five," Donna says. "If we had a larger house it would be less cluttered."

While they realize that their multiplicative style isn't for everyone, they encourage others to avoid being too safe. "You have to know what you like and who you are," Tony says. "You have to not be afraid of a pink chair."

Donna's favorite approaches include "color on the wall, area rugs, and interesting or odd lighting fixtures. I like advertising memorabilia or unusual objects in a different scale, like a giant toothbrush," she says.

"Most people who buy these houses tend to all do the same thing: brown and beige furniture and accessories from the 1960s that go with it," she continues. "I don't think that's necessary because people didn't live like that then. If you buy a book and [copy the interiors you see], it's just a paint-by-numbers approach. We visit houses like that and think, 'Yeah, it's beautiful but what part of this is the owner?'"

Ever the provocateur, Tony threatens to paint their exterior orange with purple trim. "Ain't going to happen," Donna counters with a laugh. "Or the house in a flat paint and do boomerang or sputnik stencils in gloss," he enthuses. "Then if people were walking by it would catch their eye, and they'd go, 'What was that?'"

Affordable Art

Think you can't afford original art? The Natsoulases say think again, and recommend these resources:

Craft galleries

Cheaper than fine art galleries, they're a good place to find sculptures for less.

eBay

Try keywords "modern art," "Eames paintings," or "modern paintings."

Giclee prints

Digital scans of original art printed on paper or canvas by large format printers. "You can get a giclee print for as little as $60 or $70," Tony Natsoulas says.

Student work

MFA openings at art schools and universities, and kids' exhibitions at state fairs.

Resale galleries

Artwork is typically sold on consignment and tends to be discounted.

Facing: The '60s kitchen, with its original laminate counters and recently refinished cabinets, holds an eggcup collection and miniature midcentury dollhouse appliances.

Right: Major pieces in the dining room include a linoleum sculpture near the hutch, and a wood sculpture on the table near the window wall, *Sunday Best,* both by Michael Stevens. In the backyard is Tony Natsoulas' large-scale ceramic piece, *Anthony Baltimore,* and atop the green pony wall is a lava lamp menorah by Joe Scarpa.

Kitchen **Kollectibles**

To contain a sizeable collection of housewares, this homeowner keeps many of her pieces in the built-in kitchen cupboards, rotating favorites to display throughout the house.

Jennifer and Dan Harrison's home, shown on page 124, houses a trove of vintage and retro-look kitchenware, much of which is stored in the kitchen cabinets. A room divider between the breakfast nook and the cooking triangle holds Fiesta pottery and Bauerware, as well as syrup pitchers, a canister set, and a pink breadbox. Against the plaid wallpaper inherited from the previous owners is a scalloped bookcase that holds more than two dozen Fiesta pitchers. And the tall cupboards over the Formica countertops store more Fiesta dishes, along with vintage toasters and Pyrex mixing bowls, casseroles, and refrigerator storage containers.

Jennifer began accumulating the collection about ten years ago. "At first it was mostly a tactile experience—the way a vase, bowl, or piece of pottery felt in my hands determined whether or not I brought it home. I didn't bother to look at its pattern number or manufacturer," she says. When she found that Fiestaware was such a large collecting category she decided to focus on buying a specific piece—classic disc pitchers—and limits it to just one in each of the colors or themes that appeals to her, such as Scooby Doo or yearly commemorative releases.

"Pyrex, on the other hand, I was very specific about. I remember making chocolate chip cookies in a set of bowls my mom had. I loved the bright colors and was never interested in the clear glass of the early series," she explains. "I would pick them up piece by piece really inexpensively at garage sales. It still amazes me how many complete sets I've been able to put together over the years. Those days are over, though—you can't find Pyrex at garage sales for a quarter anymore. When I started, people laughed at me

Right: A two-sided glass cabinet holds more pottery and period collectibles.

Facing: The bold colors of the dinette set and vintage signage stand out against the plaid wallpaper that came with the house. The Fiestaware disc pitchers are still being issued.

when they saw the sets and usually told me that their mom still had some in the fridge holding leftovers. Now I see Pyrex in antiques stores with prices I can't believe."

Jennifer's husband, Dan, thinks she has quite enough bowls, thank you very much, including some polka-dot Fire King ones displayed in the living room. "I really do have a lot," she admits. "In Pyrex alone, I've got close to thirty. The smaller bowls make great plate stands if you turn them upside down, and when we entertain, I love to pull out my pieces for serving and display."

There *is* one category of Pyrex you won't find at the Harrisons' house, though. "I like it up until it turns mustard and avocado; that was our childhood era. Blech!" she says. "One reason we don't like it is because it was terrible," teases Dan.

The More **the Better**

A George Nelson Marshmallow sofa upholstered in custom colors works surprisingly well with the pre-Columbian pottery displayed on a Japanese tansu chest in this 1,100-square-foot tract home.

Paul and Kathy Day believe you really can't have too much of a good thing. For them, good things include vintage midcentury pieces like an Eames DCM (Dining Chair Metal) with its original red aniline-dye finish, Danish modern furniture from Paul's youth, and a George Nelson Marshmallow sofa. Then there's the '30s French Deco pieces, Japanese tansu chests, 1920s Hawaiian koa wood souvenirs, pre-Columbian sculptures, modern kachina dolls, fly-fishing rods, Scottish tartans, Danish teak serving pieces, absinthe accoutrements, American Indian pottery, ukuleles—well you get the idea.

Outside, the couple has a collection of forty-year-old bonsai plants; a 1971 Vespa—winnowed down from half a dozen scooters; surfboards, both vintage and modern; and a 1963 Shasta trailer that they renovated inside and out in a tiki motif. Oh, and their '55 Dodge pickup is awaiting a rebuilt engine. New pieces have a place as well, such as Alessi's biomorphic kitchen accessories—corkscrews, can openers, funnels, and timers that are almost too cute to use.

Paul's family is at least in part responsible for his penchant for collecting. "They have a great eye for design," Kathy says about her in-laws, "and when they pass something down to us, it's still in the original box. If they bought it in Europe fifty years ago, or in the United States thirty years or two weeks ago—everything is complete and has directions. Paul inherited tools from his grandfather that are in seventy-year-old boxes."

Facing: In Long Beach, California, the patio between the garage and house at this Cliff May home literally works as another living space with walls or tall fences on three sides and a trellis ceiling that shades the occupants. Furnished with midcentury pieces, the minimal greenery includes potted bonsais.

Below: Miniatures, koa wood collectibles, hula girls, and a vintage radio are organized in a simple lighted bookcase.

Below right: Koa wood collectibles bearing the Hawaiian crest are displayed on a French table, and a ukulele sits on an Eames DCW (Dining Chair Wood) in this home.

"I'm the first generation that's been able to throw boxes away," Paul says brightly. When it's suggested he doesn't have room for boxes because he has so much stuff, he counters with, "Too much stuff isn't in my vocabulary. You just have to learn how to rotate your things.

"You can blame Kathy for the Vespas, our vintage fly rods, and the Shasta trailer," he continues teasingly. But Kathy explains, "What happens is I get a little idea: I'd really like a Vespa to remind me of our trips to Italy, say. Then you blink and the next thing you know, we've got eight. Such is my life."

Escape to **the Islands**

Above: Thanks to eBay, a few '50s collectibles led to this still-growing tiki collection; the homeowners try to confine it to this one room.

Facing: The former laundry room is now a full-fledged Hawaiian getaway in this Thousand Oaks, California, Eichler. Bamboo and rattan furniture, tiki mugs, masks, island art, and sea grass mats on the floor are just the beginning.

The Ferrells (see page 94 for other views of their home) took a former laundry room and turned it into an island-theme lounge—the Rincon Room—that spawned a tiki habit. Wanting a direct path from the kitchen to a new pool, the small room seemed like a good spot for a bar with wet-feet-resistant sea grass mats on the floor.

The couple already owned some rattan furniture, plus a few kitschy collectibles from the '50s, but with the purchase of *The Book of Tiki,* which "tells you everything about what happened to the tiki bars and Hawaiian restaurants that were popular in the '50s and '60s," according to Ron Ferrell, they were off. He started with tiki mugs and restaurant menus on eBay, but the sizeable collection now includes ashtrays, matchbooks, carved Oceanic Arts statues, a period-looking bar, glass fishing floats and nets on the ceiling, Hawaiian-themed art and dishes, and rustic masks.

"We can't go to Hawaii every day," says Mickee Ferrell, "but when you're sitting in the Rincon Room listening to island music and having a tropical cocktail—" "You could be in a bar in Hawaii," Ron finishes for her.

TIKI IN A NUTSHELL

In the United States in the 1920s and '30s, artistic types embraced primitivism and Hawaiian music was big on the mainland. After Prohibition ended, Don the Beachcomber and Trader Vic's were the first of the popular Polynesian-themed chain restaurants, and adding fuel to the interest in exotic food and drink were the GIs, who now wanted a piece of the islands in their basement rec rooms.

By the '50s and '60s, Hawaiian/Polynesian/tiki culture was big business, with theme restaurants, bars, motels, apartment houses, and bowling alleys, as well as Disneyland's Enchanted Tiki Room and the film *South Pacific* becoming a box-office hit.

Preserving Midcentury Neighborhoods

If you're growing alarmed at the insensitive remodels and McMansions just around the corner, here's food for thought. Historic preservation officers and homeowners from across the United States fill us in on the facts, myths, and reality of grassroots efforts.

State of the **Nation**

Above: Daly City.
Facing: Arapahoe Acres.

Postwar housing tracts are still rarely considered historic, and ranches are being torn down and replaced with lot-swallowing infill homes or remodeled into flavor-of-the-month bungaloids or hulking Tuscan villas. By virtue of their sheer numbers and relative youth, midcentury ranches aren't perceived as anything special, much less architecture that should be preserved for future generations. Even in "hot" tracts of Modernist homes, one house out of four suffers from deferred maintenance or inappropriate '80s remodeling.

"West Coast history is different, so it's easier—but still rare—for communities there to swallow the idea that something from the 1950s, especially midcentury housing, is something to preserve," says Adrian Fine, director of the Northeast Field Office of the National Trust for Historic Preservation. "In the Midwest and East Coast, it's an even harder sell. There's not a huge knowledge base for what you're losing."

In our travels for this book, the story was much the same in Colorado, Texas, Oregon, and California. We heard from homeowners in ranch neighborhoods about the slowly growing appreciation for postwar architecture, and the perceived pros and cons of historic status. It seems saving neighborhoods without losing property rights was on everyone's mind.

A few miles from San Francisco's Golden Gate Bridge, Robert Keil, a long-time resident of the Westlake neighborhood of Daly City, credits a new generation of homeowners with boosting appreciation for his quirky suburb. "There is a contingent of newcomers who clearly value the midcentury style and the durability of these homes. People e-mail our Web site wanting to know what the original exterior paint colors were and where to get floor plans so they can restore their homes properly," he says.

Houston's Memorial Bend

"One individual even wanted to know if he could join a Westlake Architectural Preservation Group, which, sadly, does not exist yet. Enough time has passed now that there is both a wide-eyed nostalgia and a genuine appreciation of these homes—something that I sense is gaining momentum."

Keil has done a lot of research into the history of his neighborhood, and speaks passionately about preserving it. "Westlake was one of the very first planned communities in the United States; it broke ground within a year of the first homes going on sale in Levittown, New York. The fact that Westlake was—and still is—a complete community of homes, schools, shopping centers, churches, offices, medical facilities, and parks, was extremely unusual and is testament to developer Henry Doelger's vision of what suburban life could be," Keil says.

"Interestingly, many developers today have repackaged this idea of community planning and have created master-planned communities or urban villages around the same principles Doelger and a few of his contemporaries espoused. But the successful postwar suburbs made this 'new' idea a living reality more than half a century ago."

A bit south of Daly City, San Jose resident Loni Nagwani, a realtor who specializes in Eichlers, declares, "I'm not into mandating architectural guidelines; I think education will do it. Five years ago, I'd sell an Eichler and the first thing they'd do was tear out the original features. Now it's a completely different ball game. The first thing they want to do is find parts and restore it. The value of Eichler owners being able to network is huge.

"HGTV has covered four Eichlers, and the Safeway [supermarket chain] contacted me because they wanted to shoot in a retro kitchen," she says. "When houses are getting to reach fifty years old, the appreciation is just beginning. The more they are written about and the more people network, the more the homes will be respected and the less we'll have to mandate design guidelines."

In Houston, architect Ben Koush doesn't mince words when talking about the lack of architectural preservation in his town. "Houston's preservation ordinance is in name only," he says. "San Antonio and Galveston and Dallas can stop you from demolishing a property or levy fines if you do, but there's not a culture of preservation here—that's why the city looks like it does. Houston had as many Victorian buildings as they do in Galveston and they're all gone, and bungalows are still being knocked down today.

"There was a French manor house from the 1920s called Dogwoods that was on a humongous property facing the bayou, and a thirty-year-old ex-Enron guy knocked it down and is going to build a 15,000-square-foot house in its place. It was on the front page of the Houston Chronicle, and people who wrote letters to the editor said things like, 'It's his property; who cares? He's improving the tax base.' It's so conservative here that you think [residents would] like their heritage, but they're more interested in property values and in doing what they want with their land," he says with exasperation.

Koush decided to do something about it and, with some like-minded Modernists, founded Houston Mod, a preservation group that hopes to capture hearts through education. "There's still a fair amount of modern architecture in Houston but it's being demolished," he says. "I think that's the most architecturally significant contribution that Houston made to popular culture, because when it was growing during the '50s, the city grew into the national consciousness. It's the fourth-largest city in the United States, and the Space Center and the Astrodome really embraced the culture of modernism. We're trying to let people know what they have and encouraging them to document their neighborhoods."

Karen Lantz, another Houston architect and midcentury ranch owner, has similar laments. "In Houston the mind-set tends to be conservative. They knocked down a three-story mall built in the 1970s," she says with some incredulity. "It just kills me that all of that building material gets thrown away."

Lantz lives in a neighborhood of modest postwar ranches that, by virtue of its location near the medical hub of the city, is seeing its share of inappro-

priate infill mansionettes. She, too, has joined the grassroots preservation group. "Houston Mod works to let people know they can renovate and restore these houses," she says. "People used to see them as throw-away homes."

Some 900 miles northwest in Englewood, Colorado, appreciation for midcentury is a bit further along. It's home to Arapahoe Acres, a tract of 124 homes built between 1949 and 1957. The work of developer Edward B. Hawkins, who designed about 100 of the ranches, and architect Eugene Sternberg, whose Bauhaus influence is seen in the economy of materials and efficient planning of the initial 20 houses, Arapahoe Acres was the first post-war district to be named to the National Register of Historic Places in 1998.

The tract's homes were set back 25 feet and sited at 23 to 45 degree angles to the street. The Modernist residences sold for between $10,000 and $20,000, and the development's model home was furnished with pieces from Eames, Nelson, Aalto, Knoll, Saarinen, and Jenneret. The original covenants, conditions, and restrictions (CC&Rs) dictated dwelling size, fences, and that

any additions must go through the architectural committee, which in reality was Hawkins himself. Paint colors are up to the homeowners, although "When in doubt, use putty"—a rule of thumb promoted by Hawkins—sums up the earth-tone palette on most Arapahoe Acres ranches.

Jim Lindberg, the director of preservation initiatives at the National Trust's Mountains/Plains office in Denver, says, "From my perspective, what's significant about Arapahoe Acres is that it was designed of a piece by an architect. It's very much a complete design, from the architecture to the landscaping to the [street] layout. If you visit you see how different that is from what's nearby—smaller, more typical gable-roofed houses from a similar period. Arapahoe Acres really stands out for their horizontal lines and siting and materials; it has a total quality that is distinctive."

About three miles away, realtor and recent midcentury convert Peter Blank, a resident of the Virginia Village/Lynwood neighborhood of Denver, does his best to educate his clients about the value of architectural originality. "I'm not about to preach to somebody what they should like or what they should do with their home, but I want the people who are purchasing these houses to understand what they're buying and how valuable it can be if they maintain the integrity," he says. "We need to try to preserve this part of Americana that's disappearing.

"The good part is, a lot of people are getting it. Ten years ago people bought here because it was affordable; it was an overlooked, neglected neighborhood. That's all changing," Blank says.

A few miles away in Littleton, Colorado, Dean Hight, a residential designer who lives in a tract called Arapaho Hills, can see both sides of the architectural preservation issue. "In our house I tried to meet our desires and requirements while retaining as much character of the neighborhood and the house that I could. This area has no covenants, and in some ways I'd like to see some because there are a lot of rundown houses," he says.

"In other ways, I don't want somebody walking around writing out tickets because I didn't put away my trash can; some people can get a little power-trippy. You have to find a happy medium. I don't necessarily want to have a homeowners' association, and I don't care to have a historic district—I don't think this neighborhood warrants it. But I would like to see people buying into it who appreciate the architecture style and want to keep it up."

Kristin Hammond and Matt Demarest have just such an association in their Portland, Oregon, ranch tract. "We're lucky that on our street there are a lot of nice homes that owners have taken care to keep true to the original style. They don't seem to want to build them out or up," Hammond says of Cedar Hills. "But there are a few two-story houses that have no business being in this neighborhood.

"I like that they don't want people storing fifth-wheels out front, but it depends on who's on the board and is calling the shots," she says. "They can interpret things and enforce whichever codes they want to."

"As far as pop-ups go, I'd rather not see that at all," Demarest adds, "but I also understand that there are people who have three or four kids in these homes who can't afford or don't want to buy a McMansion. We could raise a child in our house for a few years but then everybody would be going crazy. So, what do you do when you need more space? I just wish additions were more sensitive to the original design of the homes. I don't see that there's an aesthetic that the board is trying to endorse."

Interestingly, communities like Portland that embrace their historic buildings often don't consider postwar architecture to be meritorious. "Everyone is concerned with saving anything from the late 1800s up through World War II," says Jennifer Harrison, who recently joined the local historical society in Anaheim, California. "There's no real drive to focus on houses from the postwar boom," adds her husband, Dan. "They don't see that era as being important."

The Anaheim preservation committee got together in 1997 and deemed 1,200 structures historically significant with the cutoff year as 1949, the Harrisons explain. Jennifer says that 150 houses have been approved for California's Mills Act status—a program that grants property tax relief in ten-year increments in exchange for owners agreeing to rehabilitate and maintain their historic architecture.

"The unfortunate thing about the Mills Act is that it just applies to the front facade, so you can gut your house or have an '80s kitchen and white tile throughout the house, but if the front looks correct you qualify," Jennifer protests. Their previous house, a 1920s Anaheim bungalow, benefited from the Mills Act, but the couple's 1954 custom ranch doesn't qualify.

Still, the Harrisons are chipping away steadily at midcentury prejudice. "Anyone from the historical society who comes over loves the house," Dan says. "They recognize it as being significant. It's not a cookie-cutter home that you would have seen built in the '70s or '80s. No one gives us the impression that our house is not worth fighting to preserve. Jennifer has such strong feelings about this house and homes of this era, and she brings a fresh voice to the group. I think they want that."

"My frustration is when people talk about houses that were torn down [in the past] and they kind of have a tear in their eye. I'm looking today, right now, at cute little '50s houses that are being torn down. No one is even noticing because they're so focused on older houses," Jennifer says. "There's not a lot of 'ranch pride' around our neighborhood. When I say I have a ranch, sometimes people ask if that means I have a horse."

GROUP EFFORT

In Omaha, a spirited group of women who work in preservation by day are battling similar preconceived notions about Nebraska's postwar structures in their off hours.

"It's interesting to talk about the idea of preserving the Recent Past—fifty years doesn't seem that long ago if you're in your forties or fifties," says Cindy Tooker, an architect and a member of 2020 Omaha Modern Preservation Network.

"When I was in school, the Arts and Crafts period and even Frank Lloyd Wright weren't discussed that much because they were passé. But over the last thirty years, you see both becoming a lot more popular. First this popularity is seen in the furnishings and the clothes, where a younger generation will be attracted to that period of time," she explains. "Then it slowly progresses into the architecture. In our group we've noticed it's almost an 'Aha!' idea for people: they hadn't thought of midcentury as being old enough to be significant."

" 'Historic' in Omaha has always been 1920 or older," agrees Rebecca Kumar, a historian with the National Park Service (NPS), which oversees the National Register of Historic Places, and a 2020 Omaha member. "If it's not a brick Tudor home or a castle-esque building, it's just not historic. By selecting neon signs and a really cool pedestrian overpass in Omaha as some of our group's first preservation efforts, we were able to educate people that there are things out there other than old buildings [worth saving]. Some of the press we got was a little negative, but it also got us attention and made people go, 'Hmmm . . .' "

Carol Ahlgren, an architectural historian with NPS' National Historic Landmarks Program, is more blunt: "We just have to push the envelope on this topic. Come on people, I don't care if you remember [this architecture]; get over it. Maybe you're getting old, too."

Dena Sanford, a colleague of Ahlgren's and Kumar's at NPS, reminds us, "If you go back to the 1960s they were busy tearing down everything from the turn of the century that was considered old and ugly but not old enough yet to be historic. I tell people, 'Don't look at this from an emotional reaction of, "Oh, it's ugly!" but understand what it represents in design history. They were going for minimalism and simplicity and getting away from extraneous detail and froufrou to the core of the design.' "

The 23-member 2020 Omaha tries to be proactive in its preservation activities instead of reactive. Their advice for others looking to form a group is to spread the word with your neighbors and start with five to eight people who are willing to work, then begin surveying historic properties and start a database. Also, go into it knowing that you won't win all of your battles. In the four years since it was formed, 2020 Omaha has produced a survey of potential historic properties dating from 1920 to 1970, nominating the ones they think are most important, while educating and reaching out to city government and the public.

"Retro is so big right now, and that's one reason why younger people are getting involved in these homes and neighborhoods," says Kumar. "We've realized that there's this younger group of people that aren't just interested in architecture, but because midcentury is something cool and now, they've come to realize this is neat, well-designed architecture."

"People may be getting involved because midcentury is a fad," Sanford acknowledges, "but once they develop an appreciation for the architecture and get more involved, that interest stays."

HISTORIC PROPERTIES: FACT AND FICTION

It's a commonly held idea that nomination to the National Register of Historic Places only applies to structures fifty years old or older, and that the designation means homeowners are highly restricted on what they can and can't do to their houses. Not true, says Jeanne Lambin, a program officer at the Wisconsin Field Office of the National Trust, a private sector nonprofit advocacy group.

"A property that is younger than fifty years old can be listed on the National Register if it is of exceptional significance at the national, state, or local level. The challenge is that 'exceptional' is a relative term," she says. "And the most popular misconception is that the Feds will come in and tell people what they can and can't do with their property—what color they can paint their house, or that they'll be forced to maintain it.

"There are different levels of designation and regulation; if you live in a ranch house that's listed on the National Register, you can for the most part do

what you want as long as you're using private funds. The listing only becomes restrictive when federal money is involved or if there's a local overlay," Lambin says. "Local districts vary greatly; some are very restrictive and any changes you make have to be approved by the local preservation commission, while others are more advisory."

The NPS Web site confirms this: "Under Federal law, owners of private property listed in the National Register are free to maintain, manage, or dispose of their property as they choose, provided that there is no Federal involvement.

Owners have no obligation to open their properties to the public, to restore them or even to maintain them, if they choose not to do so."

"The issue of property owners' rights is an American thing," comments Carol Ahlgren of the NPS. "It's local laws that are more restrictive and it's also a matter of enforcement, which is only as strong as the neighborhood. It seems to me that new subdivisions' CC&Rs are more restrictive in terms of door paint colors, siding materials, and landscaping."

"A lot of people have this gut reaction: 'Oh no, don't tell me what to

Left: Arapahoe Acres' homes and overall landscaping were acknowledged as significant by the National Park Service in 1998. Its residents' willingness to uphold midcentury design principles is strictly voluntary.

Below: McMansions are the house of the moment.

do,'" Lambin agrees. "What they don't realize is that restrictive ordinances also control what your neighbors can do. That's a real benefit during this teardown craze when you don't have to worry that someone's going to demolish the house next to you, remove all of the trees from the lot, and put up this monster house."

THE VALUE OF PRESERVATION

All over the United States, residents are shaking their heads over the McMansions that are replacing small original homes, but the trend shows no sign of slowing down. "The average house size keeps getting bigger across the country; that's not changing. If you look at popular culture, HGTV and other home makeovers are promoting the idea of spending money on your house—getting the great room, getting the big garage, all of these features," says the National Trust's Adrian Fine. "That's what people are focusing on today and it's likely to continue for some time."

Architectural historian Carol Ahlgren reminds us that we're members of a larger tribe. "It's not just your house, although that's what we think. Part of what makes your house special is that it's part of a neighborhood and you are one owner in a much larger whole. Respecting that in terms of setback, materials, and sensitivity to the street and the neighborhood when you're considering adding on or a remodel [is vital]," she says.

"A friend lives in Bethesda in a neighborhood of simple postwar and Modernist houses. People have started buying them, tearing them down and throwing up McMansions," she continues. "It's almost painful to see a house that's so wrong and does not belong there."

Architect Cindy Tooker agrees. "In Nebraska we see classic raised ranches all of a sudden being overpowered by a four-story Tudor revival a la 1999. The '50s house and its little carport now get no sun."

"People don't consider these neighborhoods to be historic and don't have any ordinances in place," Ahlgren adds. "Not everything is architect designed. Simpler vernacular buildings may not jump out and grab you, but as part of a district or collection, they make a statement about the era and the design and what it represented in people's lives."

But convincing people that midcentury is historic takes grit, vision, and charm. "History doesn't stop at 1945; these types of neighborhoods contribute just as much as those from the 1920s or any other residential period," Fine says. "The diversity of the architecture is what makes most communities rich and interesting.

"You don't want to wake up and realize you have nothing left from the '50s because it wasn't the primo Eichler- or Williams-designed ranch development. The Recent Past isn't always pretty. It may not be the most aesthetically pleasing houses or subdivisions, but the story behind them might be really compelling and interesting and you may not even be aware of it."

The way to help curb teardowns is by banding together, Fine says. Find out if others in your town are similarly concerned; reach out to decision makers, and work to build a collective community voice on preservation priorities. Also be prepared to compromise—stopping teardowns entirely is unlikely.

At dozens of town hall meetings and other planning sessions where Fine talks with residents about preservation and teardown concerns, he's developed some persuasive arguments. "Teardowns are mostly about short-term gains: look at all the new investment, look at the tax revenue is very short sighted. The long-term implications are about aesthetics, losing historic architecture, and about that starter house that will no longer exist in your community," he says. "It's also about there becoming one socioeconomic class in your community if teardowns continue. People of middle- and low-income means can't afford to get into the market once teardowns take over.

"The people who are cashing out and selling their houses are making large sums of money and more often than not, they're moving elsewhere. They are leaving you with the problems. There are communities in Texas where at least 50 percent of the original housing stock has been replaced," Fine continues. "Hinsdale, outside of Chicago, is kind of a poster child—it has lost about 40 percent of its original homes. And Denver is losing around one hundred bungalows a year.

"Are these neighborhoods and communities places you're going to want to live ten, fifteen years from now? They're not going to look the same, and they're not going to have the same people. Preservation is about making hard decisions today so the community you care about will be something like what it is today—tomorrow."

"Our 1950s and '60s suburban architecture is worth preserving because it was the product of a pivotal time period and represented a permanent change in the way Americans lived," Daly City resident Rob Keil philosophizes. "That suburban lifestyle remains dominant sixty years later.

"These modest homes were the fulfillment of the American middle-class dream, bringing a higher standard of living to average people, and giving birth to a whole new way of life. There is a type of beauty in their simplicity, their efficient use of space, and the creativity with which they employed inexpensive materials to deliver a modern look," he continues. "One Westlake architect told me, 'It's easy to do award-winning architecture with unlimited time and unlimited budgets, but when you deal with constraints and you still manage to do something beautiful, that's a real accomplishment.'

"When architecture grows out of the real needs of society and improves people's lives on an everyday basis, that's something worth preserving."

RANCH RESOURCES

Books & publications

Atomic Ranch quarterly magazine:
www.atomic-ranch.com

The Book of Tiki, by Sven Kirsten, Taschen

Eichler Homes: Design for Living, by Jerry Ditto,
Chronicle Books

Eichler: Modernism Rebuilds the American Dream, by
Paul Adamson, Gibbs Smith, Publisher

The Ranch House, by Alan Hess, Harry N. Abrams,
Inc., Publisher

Ranch House Style, by Katherine Ann Samon, Clarkson
Potter/Publishers

Western Ranch Houses by Cliff May, Sunset
Magazine and Books, Hennessey + Ingalls

Select midcentury & preservation Web sites

2020 Omaha Modern Preservation Network:
www.2020omaha.org

Arapahoe Acres: www.arapahoeacres.org

California Mills Act:
http://ohp.parks.ca.gov/default.asp?page_id=2
1412

Cliff May/The Ranchos: www.ranchostyle.com

Thomas Church: http://lakewold.org/tchurch.html

Daly City/Westlake:
www.westlakehistory.org,
www.kevingardiner.com/westlake.html

Eichler Homes:
www.eichlernetwork.com, www.eichlersocal.com

Frank Lloyd Wright Usonian Houses:
www.bc.edu/bc_org/avp/cas/fnart/fa267/FL
W_usonian.html

Garrett Eckbo: www.gardenvisit.com/b/eckbo.htm

Houston Mod: www.houstonmod.org

Levittown, New York:
http://tigger.uic.edu/~pbhales/Levittown

Lotta Livin': www.lottaliving.com

Lustron Homes:
http://members.tripod.com/~Strandlund/index-
5.html, http://home.earthlink.net/~ronusny

Memorial Bend, Houston:
http://users.ev1.net/~michaelb/bend/bend-
home.htm

National Registry of Historic Places:
www.cr.nps.gov/nr

National Trust for Historic Preservation:
www.nationaltrust.org

Palm Springs Modern Committee:
www.psmodcom.com

Palm Springs Modernism Show:
www.palmspringsmodernism.com

Recent Past Preservation Network:
www.recentpast.org

Streng Bros. homes:
www.eichlernetwork.com/streng.html

Featured furnishings & accessories

Alessi: www.alessi.com

Atwater Pottery: www.atwaterpottery.com

B&B Italia: www.bebitalia.it

Boomerang for Modern:
www.boomerangformodern.com

Copenhagen Furniture:
www.copenhagenfurniture.com

Crate & Barrel: www.crateandbarrel.com

Dania Home and Office: www.daniafurniture.com

Design Within Reach: www.dwr.com

InterfaceFLOR: www.interfaceflor.com

Go-Kat-Go: www.go-kat-go.com

Herman Miller: www.hermanmiller.com

Highbrow, Inc.: www.highbrowfurniture.com

Hive: www.hivemodern.com

House Industries: www.houseindustries.com

IKEA: www.ikea-usa.com

Knoll International: www.knoll.com

Metro Retro: www.metroretrofurniture.com

Mitchell Gold + Bob Williams:
www.mitchellgold.com

Modernica: www.modernica.net

Natuzzi: www.natuzzi.com

Out of Vogue: www.outofvogue.com

Plummers Home and Office:
www.plummersfurniture.com

Pottery Barn: www.potterybarn.com

Pure Design: www.puredesignonline.com/collection

Restoration Hardware: www.restorationhardware.com

Retromodern: www.retromodern.com

Room & Board: www.roomandboard.com

Scandinavian Designs Home and Office:
www.scandinaviandesigns.com

Todd Oldham for La-Z-Boy: www.lazboy.com

Featured appliances & fixtures

Agape: www.agapedesign.it

Amana: www.amana.com

Artemide: www.artemide.com

Asko: www.askousa.com

Blanco America: www.blancoamerica.com

Bosch: www.boschappliances.com

Broan: www.broan.com

Dacor: www.dacor.com

DCS: www.dcsappliances.com

Dornbracht: www.dornbracht.com

Droog: www.droogdesign.nl

Frigidaire: www.frigidaire.com

Frontier Cabinets: www.frontiercabinets.com

General Electric: www.ge.com

Grohe: www.grohe.com

Jenn-Air: www.jennair.com

KitchenAid: www.kitchenaid.com

Lite Line Illuminations: www.halogenlighting.com

Lux: www.luxlights.com

Marvel: www.lifeluxurymarvel.com

Maytag: www.maytag.com

Stanford Electric Works:
Palo Alto, California, 650.323.4139

Target: www.target.com

Thermador: www.thermador.com/home.cfm

Traulsen: www.traulsen.com

Featured architectural elements

CaesarStone: www.caesarstoneus.com

Cesar cabinets: http://www.cesar.it/index1.html

Cement counters: Cheng Concrete Exchange:
www.concreteexchange.co

Expo Design Center: www.expo.com

Formica: www.formica.com

Hermosa Terrazzo: www.hermosati.com

Home Depot: www.homedepot.com

Marmoleum: www.themarmoleumstore.com

Nana Wall: www.nanawall.com

Nickels Custom Cabinets: www.nickelscabinets.com

RAM Industries windows:
Stafford, Texas, 281.495.9056

SileStone: www.silestoneusa.com

Featured architects, interior designers & landscape designers

Kathleen Ferguson Landscapes:
www.kathleenferguson.com

Paula Hanson, Terra Bella Landscape Design:
www.terrabellalandscape.com

Dean Hight Design:
Littleton, Colorado, 303.523.4796

Mark Houston Associates, Inc.:
Monrovia, California, 626.357.7858

Catherine Johnson, Johnson Blohm Associates:
Houston, Texas, 713.961.9816

Patrick Killen, Christian Navar, STUDIO 9 ONE 2:
www.studio9one2.com

Karen Lantz, Enter Architecture:
www.enterarchitecture.com

Featured artwork

Robert Arneson:
www.briangrossfineart.com/artists/rarneson

Heidi Bekebrede: www.cuteware.net

Jeff Bertoncino:
www.bogenagalerie.com/Artists/Bertoncino/
Bertoncino.php

Lisa Fournier: lisafournierart@msn.com

David Gilhooly: www.davidgilhooly.com

Judy Gittelsohn Paintings: www.judyg.com

Arthur Gonzalez:
www.natsoulas.com/html/artists/arthurGonzalez
/arthurGonzalez.html

Peter Illig: www.peterillig.com

Anthony Natsoulas: www.tonynatsoulas.com

Jeff Nebeker:
www.sdgallery.com/catalogs/nebeker/gallery

Oceanic Arts: www.oceanicarts.net

Michael Stevens:
www.crockerartmuseum.org/exhibitions/
exhib_pages/Knock_on_Wood.htm

ACKNOWLEDGMENTS

Our thanks to some all-important people who helped make this book possible: Elizabeth Brown, Cheyenne Wortham, Barret Neville, and Carrie Westover at Gibbs Smith. Also thanks to Clyde Mannon and Michael O'Neal for their archival materials, and all of the homeowners and enthusiasts who shared their midcentury marvels with us and our readers.